# The Web Content Strategist's Bible

The Complete Guide to a New and Lucrative Career Path
for Writers of All Kinds

## Richard Sheffield

CLUEfox Publishing – Atlanta, GA - 2009
First paperback edition 2009

This book includes information from many sources and gathered from my personal experiences. It is published as a general reference and not intended to substitute for independent verification by readers where necessary and appropriate. The publisher and author disclaim any personal liability, directly or indirectly, for advice or information presented within. Although the author and publisher have prepared this manuscript with utmost care and diligence, we assume no responsibility for errors, inaccuracies, omissions, or inconsistencies.

**Attn: Quantity discounts are available to your company, educational institution, or writing organization**

For more information contact the publisher, CLUEfox Publishing at this email address – **cluefox@gmail.com**

**CLUEfox Publishing**

This book is dedicated to my parents and grandparents who made sure that, if I learned nothing else in school, I learned how to write.

# Acknowledgements

Thanks to my bosses and co-workers at KnowledgeWare who let me run with my crazy ideas about putting reference information up on the then, brand new Web.

Thanks to everyone I worked with at IBM's Interactive Design Studio and Art's Café where we got to push the idea that this is REALLY not your father's IBM!

Thanks to everyone at UPS for allowing me to put to work all the things I had learned about content strategy.

A special thanks goes to Dr. Margaret Walters and Dr. Sarah Robbins for all kinds of help.

# Contents

# Tables

# Figures

# Introduction

Life at the bottom of the food chain is no fun for anyone. It doesn't matter if you are a mouse or a writer, being overlooked, ignored, and utterly dispensable is frustrating. Now, everyone hold on a minute before you start writing me hateful emails; I know all the arguments. I was a tech writer for eleven years. It was a good job and I had a lot of great experiences, but I still felt like I was at the bottom of the hierarchy. I talked constantly about how I was the first advocate for the user and the first system tester. I know that I made countless user interface change suggestions and that the ultimate user experience was better because I was on the team. I was a very good technical writer and no one argued that fact. But my opinion was still perceived as less important than the other members of the development team. I could suggest changes, but others had to actually make them, and often took credit for them as well. I felt underpaid, under-appreciated, overworked, and unfulfilled.

Even though I had been working in the software development world for much longer than many of the programmers and designers with whom I was teamed, and I encountered the same problems over and over again and often knew we were headed down the wrong road, usually all I could do was say, "I told you so," when things went badly. Don't get me wrong; I was not a shy guy. I stated my case well and with conviction. It was just that no one really had to listen to, or take advice from, the tech writer. It's as simple as that.

So I walked away from a stable, yet dull, job I had held for years and decided to do some technical writing contract work to see how things worked elsewhere. Unfortunately, I found only more of the same or worse. My co-workers were even *less* likely to be interested in what I had to say because I was a contractor. I knew my job, was damn good at it, and by this point in my career I felt like I could make a strong contribution at a higher, more strategic, level in a project. But this was a sand box in which tech writers were just not allowed to play. It didn't matter how much experience I had.

Eventually I landed at IBM. The Internet was exploding and IBM was just getting into the whole Web design thing. The Web development team needed someone to set up a technical writing department, providing technical documentation for the websites they were building for big Fortune 500 customers. Part of what they needed to provide as part of a website launch project was information on how to boot and take down the servers and how to upload new files, etc. It was a good gig, but the managers had a hard time finding a home for me in the organization. The technical manager didn't want me, as he only managed programmers. So I was placed with the only other writers in the group—the Web copy writers and the content strategists—a group whose title I did not yet understand.

I went about my job mixed in with these others writers whose jobs seemed much more interesting and creative than mine. They wrote Web copy for the new websites that the group was developing and also wrote and helped design the detailed and very creative proposals that they sent out to clients to try and win new business. Little by little, I began to infiltrate their work world. First, by writing and editing the technical portions of the proposal documents we were sending out, then later by actually helping out with developing creative ideas for new Web content.

The more involved I got, the more it became obvious that these other writers had a much better job than I did. They went to off-site meetings and talked about wild and creative ideas, and everyone listened to them. Shocking! Their ideas went up on the white board and got considered along with all the others. And they got to talk to actual customers! I had been in software development for eleven years and never met a single customer; yet these guys were flying all over the country to meet with clients all the time. This was unheard of in my world. Something interesting was happening here.

# The Day I Doubled My Salary

I was ready to make my move. I spent days writing out my accomplishments, listing the projects to which I had made significant contributions, printing out sample documents, and finding complimentary emails from clients and team members. I walked to my boss's office armed and ready to do battle.

"Hiya. Got a few minutes to talk about some stuff?"

"Sure," she said. "Come on in."

"Well I've been working a lot on Web content projects and helping out where I can. My tech writing material is well defined now and I could easily hand it off to someone else. So... I was wondering if I could change to a content strategist role?" I opened up my folder, ready to provide all kinds of back-up documentation.

"Sure, great! Do you want to start now or in the morning? I have a few projects I can assign to you right now."

I was shocked! It was as simple as that. All I had to do was ask. No long negotiations and proving my ability. She already knew me, she had work that needed doing, and she was happy to have me step up and take it on. I quickly found myself on a plane to New York City to meet with PriceWaterhouseCoopers about phase two of a project we had just launched for them. And shortly after that, I was off to spend nine months in Paris working on another project. All paid for by the client. Why didn't I ask for this job sooner!

All this time, I was still on contract. My contract rate got a nice bump and I was quite happy with things. But it was not too long before IBM wanted to hire me as a full-time employee. Again, I was shocked. The offer they gave me was a lot more than I was making on contract, and fully twice as much as I had ever made on salary as a tech writer.

## Maybe All You Need to Do Is Ask

I mention my easy path into the Web development world not to brag, but because it was all there, right in front of me, and all I had to do was ask. Eighty percent of my skills and experience translated well to this new job, and the things I had to learn were actually fun and creative. I didn't mind putting in the extra work and extra time because I really enjoyed getting up and going to work in the morning! Without even knowing it, you may be in a similar situation. If you have good writing and editing skills, you are a seasoned Web user and are interested in how websites are developed, and you know how to manage a project through to completion, all you may have to do is ask.

## Is "Web Content Strategist" a Real Job?

Yes, it absolutely is. However, you could work an entire career as a writer and never even hear this job title unless you work directly in website development. This is a growth field as both large companies who manage their own websites, and Web agencies need content strategists. But you don't have to take my word for it. As I am writing this, I just went out to Monster.com and got 35 results when I searched for the keywords "web, content, strategist." One of the jobs listed a top-end salary of $105,00.00! Here a composite ad I created based on what I just found online to give you an example of what companies are looking for. I have a list of other typical Web Content Strategist duties and responsibilities in Appendix B of this book.

**Web Content Strategist**

The Content Strategist is responsible for overseeing all content requirements, and creating all content strategy deliverables (content audits, gap analyses, taxonomies, metadata frameworks, content style guides, content migration plans, etc.) across the project lifecycle. Collaborating closely with the Information Architect, Taxonomy Lead, internal business clients and people from our Editorial, Creative, Strategy and Technology groups, you will be critical to defining the content quality, processes and workflows for the websites and applications our teams create. You will also work closely with the clients to ensure the necessary content is generated using best practices and the methodologies you set up. Ideal candidates will have a healthy sense of humor, and an ability to collaborate and inform without needing to be the smartest person in the room.

## Position Description

Responsibilities include:

- Consulting with sales and internal business stakeholders to understand and assess their needs relative to the Sales Portal and recommend appropriate solutions
- Determining projects' overall content requirements and potential content source
- Review content with owners and validate the following: appropriate channel, audience, role, and timing
- Enter content into the Content Management System and publish to the portal
- Pro-actively reach out to coordinators and business stakeholders to assist with content accuracy and "freshness"
- Equal fluency in techno-speak and layman's terms
- Participate in additional projects, including portal release cycles and process and communication redesign initiatives
- Establishing a style guide and editorial procedures for all written elements of the site

## Minimum Requirements

- 5+ years experience with process, communications, operations, project management, and/or web technology and content management tools from an operations perspective.
- Knowledge of web content and development processes, best practices, and emerging trends
- Excellent project management skills with demonstrated ability to implement
- Customer-oriented
- Proficient in MS Office applications, and experience with content management systems
- Demonstrated experience working with sales organizations, processes, and systems
- Experience with Vignette Content Management System or Portal, is a plus
- Excellent organization, interpersonal, written, and verbal communication skills are essential
- Ability to work and negotiate with all levels of individuals within the organization in a project environment
- Demonstrated team facilitation and problem solving skills
- Excellent relationship building and coordination skills
- Ability to work in a team environment under tight deadlines with multiple concurrent deliverables
- Has a "does what it takes" attitude in accomplishing tasks to meet deadlines

- Self-motivated and quick learner

## Additional Knowledge & Skills

- Knowledge of web content and development processes, best practices, and emerging trends
- Excellent project management skills with demonstrated ability to implement
- Customer-oriented
- Proficient in MS Office applications, and experience with content management systems

## Education

Requires a Bachelor's Degree or equivalent experience

Note that this job description sounds very specific and has a lot of requirements that you might not think you have. I know nothing about the company and only the basics about the position, but I can almost guarantee that the hiring manager would ignore most of these "requirements" if he was talking to someone with decent writing experience and project management skills. What any company mainly wants when looking to hire a content strategist is:

- A decent writer and editor

- Someone who understands how to plan and implement a project

- Someone who really wants to do this kind of work

- Someone who understands the bare basics of how the Web works technically

The rest is all gravy. Everyone is "customer-focused" and has a "does what it takes" attitude. Be personable, smart, pleasant to work with, and show that you have those four items listed above and very few content strategist jobs will be impossible to get. Add that you have some knowledge about content management systems that we will cover later in the book and you will be golden.

# What Is Web Content?

So when I'm talking about a Web content strategist and Web content projects, just what am I talking about? This is actually not a trivial question, and the answer may vary depending upon whom you are talking to. Technically, Web content can be anything that appears on a website, including words, pictures, video, sounds, downloadable files (PDF), buttons, icons, and logos. For the discussions in this book, when I refer to Web content, I'm usually talking about the editorial content—the paragraphs, sentences, and words on a Web page. A content strategist may be involved in tracking and locating some of these other types of content, but for the most part, we will be talking about the processes surrounding the identification, creation, and approval of the words on the page.

Other types of Web content will be covered individually as they come up. But let's not oversimplify this either. As Web users have become more and more sophisticated, their expectations for Web content have become higher. Just having a lot of content is no longer enough. The content has to be well organized (this is usually the information architect's job) and it must hang together in a coherent way and communicate value and a good story (this is the content strategist's job).

Editorial content becomes more than just words on a page. As a content strategist, you will also need to consider:

---

- **How is this information relevant to what the user is doing?** A user who is just beginning to think about buying a product needs very different information than someone who has done a lot of research and just wants detailed specifications. These users have different criteria for what relevant product information might be. This is often referred to as the user's context in the site.

- **Is the content comprehensive?** Is everything present on the site that a user might want to know so they can successfully accomplish whatever they came to the website to accomplish?

- **Is the content appropriately labeled and defined?** These labels and definitions of the content are referred to as metadata—data about data. Keywords or tags for searching might be metadata, as could a list of countries for which the content is appropriate. Metadata makes the content able to be manipulated automatically by computer systems based on business rules. For instance, products labeled as "book" should only appear in certain areas of the site.

- **What is the most efficient way to develop this content?** Ultimately, someone is going to have to write, import, or copy and paste existing text into some kind of data repository for the site, usually a Web content management system (WCMS) of some sort. What tools will be used? What workflows and approvals are needed? If there is a WCMS, how easy are the input forms to use and should the content strategist help design them? Is there enough time in the project plan to create all the needed content? The team will look to the content strategist to help answer these questions.

All of these elements become as much a part of the Web editorial content as the words and sentences.

## Working In the Web Design World

What I found out very quickly is that working in the Web design and development world is very different from working in software development. I had serious culture shock. The kind of work is very different, the level of exposure is much greater, and there is a whole new cast of characters with whom you will have to learn to work.

The Web design and development world is divided into two groups: in-house development groups, and Web agencies. In-house teams work for a company and take care of its website. They work on the same site all the time. An example would be Amazon. It has a large internal Web development team that does most of the work on Amazon.com. Web agencies like Razorfish or Sapient work on lots of different websites.

The kind of work done is pretty much the same between in-house groups and agencies. The big difference is that agencies have to do a lot of work on proposals and selling to get new clients and new work. In-house groups don't have this problem, but they have to have a process to prioritize possible projects and decide what to work on next. The kinds of jobs and roles are pretty similar in both groups.

## What Are the Projects and Who Are the Players?

In the Web design world, work is divided up into projects. There are a lot of different kinds of possible projects, but most of them fall into one of these broad groups:

- **New Websites** – There are fewer of these kinds of projects than there used to be. Most companies already have a website at this point so most of the brand new sites are for brand new companies. These are big projects that have large budgets and take a long time to complete. The content development effort is substantial.
- **New Mini-site Development** – Website owners often have content that is just needed for a short duration for a specific product launch or campaign. In this case, they may choose to not place the content inside their larger website, but to create a small site that they can direct customers to while the campaign is running and that can be easily removed once it is over. These sites often have a short, easy-to-remember URL that is

referred to as a "vanity" URL. For lots of Web agencies, these sites make up a large portion of their project load. These projects almost always need completely new content written and have tight deadlines to match a product launch or ad campaign.

• **Existing Website Re-design** – There are a lot of websites out there that are starting to show their age. The look and feel of a website and common user expectations have changed a lot since many of these sites were created, so there is a lot of work to be done completely redesigning and re-launching existing, out-of-date websites. Despite the fact that there is existing editorial content for these sites, quite often the new design will force much of the content to be re-written and reformatted. These are big projects that often get lumped in with developing new features and improving the technical architecture of the site.

• **New Web Application Development** – Most pages on the Web are what is known as static content. These pages just display words and graphics for the user to read and view. Web applications are Web pages that accept some kind of input from the user and/or then return something to the user. For example, features like online shopping, or online bill pay are Web applications. They are computer programs that live in a Web page. This is also very popular now as companies try to find way to keep customers on the site longer. This kind of work is done both in-house and by Web agencies. The content needs for these projects usually include text for help pop-ups and other page content surrounding the application itself, as well as any text needed inside the application.

Web application development projects are usually large and complex projects with lots of people moving in and out as needed. Every project has different needs, but most have someone acting in these kinds of roles:

- **Sponsor/Client** – This is the person who is paying the bills and who ultimately will accept or reject the entire project. For an in-house development group, the sponsor/client is the person who is sponsoring the project, usually an executive, and this person is the one you have to keep happy. This is the person you go to in order to get the final answer to questions about requirements. It is critical to establish just who is in charge.

- **Project Manager** – Sometimes also referred to as a Producer (though a Producer may have more financial responsibilities), the project manager (or PM) creates the project plan and tracks tasks performed by all the people involved. Each group (technical, design, content) may have its own, detailed plan, but the PM keeps up with big project milestones to make sure that everything is running on time and that the project will be delivered within the terms of the contract, or requirements. They usually schedule meetings, keep track of issues, coordinate between departments, report up to clients and senior management, and generally make sure that everything is moving forward. Project managers are very busy people.

• **Art Director** – Sometimes this person may be called a Creative Director. The Art Director's job is to design and create, or oversee the creation of, the graphical look and feel of the site. These people pick the color pallet, and design how the pages look and fit in with the client's existing brand, and brand standards. They will work on the project very early to create examples of how the site might look (comps) so the customer can select a look they want. Once development begins, this person is usually just involved as graphical design problems come up during programming and testing.

• **Technical Lead** – This person might also be called a Technical Architect. This person's job is to plan and oversee all of the technical parts of the project such as server software selection, hosting, programming languages, etc. If a new content management system is being developed as part of the project, the content strategist would be spending a lot of time with the technical lead.

• **Information Architect** – The information architect (or IA) is responsible for designing how the user moves around the site and how the information is arranged and displayed. IAs design the site navigation structure (which pages link to which other pages) and usually design the user interface for any Web applications. IAs are sometimes called User Experience Architects or experts. The IAs are usually on the critical path for the project, other things cannot be done until they complete their work. Often there is some overlap between what the IA does and what a content strategist could do.

• **Content Strategist** – Obviously we will spend the rest of the book talking about the roles and responsibilities of a content strategist, but the short description is that this person is responsible for estimate, planning, tracking, and overseeing the development, translation, and approval for all the editorial content on the site. This process may involve everything from information about the company and its management, to thousands of product description pages, one for every item the company sells.

A content strategist will have to deal with all of the people and roles listed above at various times in the project cycle. Of all of these people, the most important in the content strategist's life is usually the information architect. Establishing a good relationship with the IA at the start of a project will make everything easier and more enjoyable. The next chapter has a whole section on how to figure out who does what when there are conflicts with the IA.

# A Day In the Life of a Web Content Strategist

There are two things that I know for sure about working as a Web content strategist:

- No two days are the same.
- You will rarely get into a rut.

The problems to be solved and challenges to overcome will be different for every project. You will not be spending many days behind a computer all day long. Sure, there will be a few dull days here and there, but Web content strategy is an interactive job and you function as part of a team. So there will be lots of meetings for planning, creating strategy, and problem solving.

So here are a few of the kinds of things you might be doing in a day on the job as a Web content strategist:

- Design reviews for a future project that is still in planning and meet with the designers and information architects to learn about a new project that needs your editorial input.
- Write content for a project that is currently in production. This is a project with a deadline, so you would have certain writing and editing tasks assigned to you to perform.

- Track writing work to be done by others for another project on which you are working. In this project, some of the writing is to be done by the client's marketing department. You have given the content authors in the marketing department a list of exactly what needs to be written and a schedule of when things are due. One of your tasks is to track their work and make sure they are on schedule.
- Perform Search Engine Optimization keyword research.
- Use other sources like Forrester Research to find trends or material that will help get further insight into this sector or audience.
- Attend problem-solving meetings. Clients just added new requirements for another project your team is working on. Now they also want all the content to be translated into Spanish. You meet with the rest of the team to figure out what the new content development process will be and how long this will take. You come up with an estimate to take back to the client. Doing the translations in the current project will add a significant amount of time and delay the product launch. You recommendation is to perform this work as a phase-two project to be started as soon as the current project launches.
- Edit the work of others as newly-written Web content comes to you in the Web content management system. You have a number of copy writing contractors working on several projects.

One of your tasks is to edit their work to make sure your editorial style guide is followed.

This is just a small list of possible things you might be called upon to do, but you can see the tasks are varied and interesting.

## Does This Sound Interesting to You?

I know a lot of these ideas may be new to you if you have not worked a lot on the Web. The most important ideas to take away from this section are that Web content strategist is a real job, it pays well, and it's not rocket science. You do not have to be a programmer or know HTML.

If you are interested in planning writing projects, you enjoy thinking about how to best help the client communicate with the reader, and you like working on the Web, then read on. I hope to open up a whole new career field for you.

The Web Content Strategist's Bible

# Chapter 1 – An Introduction to Web Content Strategy

## What Is Web Content Strategy?

Content strategy is a repeatable system that defines the entire editorial content development process for a website development project, from very early tasks such as analyzing and classifying readers to the very last tasks, such as planning for the ongoing content maintenance after the project launches. The content strategist's job is to:

- Make sure that every block of content on the proposed site, from marketing content to copyright statements in the footer, is recorded, accounted for, assigned, and tracked.
- Assign a specific person (not a department) for creation, editing, copy approval, translation, translation approval, legal approval, metadata definition, electronic storage and retrieval, and periodic review for each content item.
- Track the ongoing progress of each task.
- Create, and get approval for, contingency plans for major content milestones.

- Train and supervise the content staff and possibly create an editorial style guide for Web content if none exists.
- Work with the technical leads to represent the end users when creating Web Content Management Systems, templates, and automated workflows.

The business justification for having someone in this role is that by including an editor/writer in the role of Content Strategist at the beginning of the project you will get:

- Better estimates
- Better project plans
- More control of the project during implementation
- A firmer foundation based upon research and analysis that supports the IA and technology recommendations to ensure ROI

A complete content strategy translates into more accurate contracts and more profitable, and cost effective projects. As a result, content strategists get paid more than Web copywriters and stay on a project longer. If you get paid by the hour, this is a very good thing!

The rest of this book will focus on these tasks in detail and give you the tools (documents and spreadsheets) needed to perform these tasks in the context of a website development project. So don't worry too much at this point about how you are going to accomplish these tasks. Just get a feel for the kinds of things you might be asked to do as a Web content strategist and the kinds of tasks that will be within your area of responsibility.

# The Origins of Content Strategy

In 1995, there were one-person website development companies all over the place. Back then it was possible for one person to program the site, create a few images (usually a logo), copy some content from an existing brochure, create a home page and maybe five or ten other pages and host the whole thing—and do all this in less than a week.

But as users got more sophisticated, so did website development. The first area of specialization became graphic design. Websites began to have more of a graphical impact, rather than just words on a page, so graphic designers began to specialize in Web development. Programmers began to specialize, and eventually things got so complicated that a whole new career was born, the information architect (IA). An IA's job is to figure out how all of the site fits together in a well-defined hierarchical navigational structure and to plan the entire user experience on the site. At first, the IA's had a hard time being recognized as having a valid job function, but over time clients saw the value in what the IAs did and now they are very valuable team members. Really good IAs take home big pay checks. Content strategists face the same issues today.

Everything was coded in HTML so a few copywriters might be needed, but they didn't really need any special skills other than knowledge of Microsoft Word. But as Web professionals learned more about how people actually were using the Web, it became clear that how the editorial content was structured and worded mattered a

---

great deal. Text written in a certain manner was much more easily understood by the reader online.

About the same time, Web developers started noticing that all these sites they had created were really hard to change and maintain because the site code was all mixed in with the site textual content. Changing the graphical look of a site became a nightmare because the HTML tags for how the text was displayed were all mixed in with the words. So new Web Content Management Systems (WCMS) were created so that an author could write, save, and edit the website's text separately from what the designer was doing to define the website's look and feel. But now all the authors had to become experts in using these complicated systems.

Also at about the same time, website development projects started to get really big and complicated and they were often being delivered late. Sometimes they were really late. Studies were done, experts were called in, and one of the most common reasons for a late project was that the content was late. Developing, approving, translating, and getting everything into the WCMS, and then out of the WCMS and tested took much longer than anyone had planned on. Generally this was because this task had been very poorly estimated and poorly planned.

Suddenly there was a need for someone to oversee the content development process, understand the WCMS, guide the copywriters, track all of the content being created, set and enforce standards, and create content development plans based on how long the work was really going to take, not a wish and a hope. Enter the Web

---

The Web Content Strategist's Bible

content strategist. Just as the IA's had to fight to prove their worth, content strategists had to fight the same battle.

# Web Content Strategist vs. Information Architect

Most of the current overlap seems to be between the content strategist's role and the IA's role. Could some of the things that a content strategist does be done by an IA? Sure. But the real question is *should they*? IA's deal with a lot of the same issues and those with an interest in writing often do a fine job at developing the content strategy, but they are a scarce resource. No organization that I know of has too many IAs.

Most of the conflict happens during the early phases of a project when the user experience is being designed and the structure set. Most content strategists don't want to step over onto the IA's turf, but there are things they can help with and might actually do better than the IA. I frequently have IAs come to me for help with naming, categorization, nomenclature, and navigational issues.

This is really a situation that will have to be handled on a project-by-project basis for the foreseeable future. Every case will be different depending upon the players. Every IA is not the same and does not have the same skill set. Some IAs are former programmers, some are former technical writers, and many are now coming out of design schools and library science programs. They have different strengths and weaknesses. Plus, some projects are very content-heavy and some are not. There seems to be plenty of work for people in both roles.

So the current argument is to put the IAs to work on new design projects as quickly as possible doing what they do best and let a content strategist handle as much of the content work as can be offloaded. One day a good Web content strategist will be just as highly valued as a good IA.

## Who Could be a Web Content Strategist?

All of the content strategists I know (including myself) stumbled into the field by complete accident. Content strategists I know have backgrounds in:

- Technical writing
- Advertising copywriting
- Programming
- Screen writing
- Print journalism
- Broadcast journalism
- Project management
- Direct mail copywriting
- Business management
- Television production

That's probably just a start. What they all share is an interest in writing, an interest in contributing on a strategic level to a project, the ability to be proactive, and a strong interest in the Web. Everything else can be learned. One of the best content strategists I know had never even used an Excel spreadsheet and had no technical background at all. She could barely spell HTML and had no idea what it meant. These things can be learned if you have the other skills and the ability to pick things up as you go along.

One of the most important characteristics of a good content strategist is the ability to be proactive. If you want to sit back and wait for someone to tell you what to do, then this is not a job for you. Good content strategists run the show. They anticipate problems, and constantly look for ways to do things better. They are out in front dealing with problems and with the customers. The rest of the team treats them as an equal development partner and pays attention to what they say.

# The Website Development Process

Just as there are many different ways to develop a software product, no two groups use the exact same process to create a website. But there are a lot of similarities, and Web development teams all go through very similar steps. Different groups just give them different names and perhaps use different techniques. Every development group or agency has its own methodology. Methodology is just a fancy consultant word for a repeatable process. First they do X then Y then Z.

In one form or another, Web development teams all go through the following phases and each phase will be discussed in detail in subsequent chapters:

- **Proposal Phase** – Sometimes called Phase Zero, this is all the stuff that happens before a project is given the go-ahead and work begins. In an agency this is usually a response to a request from a potential customer for a proposal. As a content strategist, you might be called upon to help write the proposal, but most agencies have boilerplate text that they use over and over again in proposals to clients.

In a corporate environment, there is some process used to collect and evaluate potential Web projects. All the requested projects are ranked by some method (branding impact, marketing campaign support, potential return on investment, etc.) and then some projects are given the go-ahead. In a corporate environment, a content strategist may be called upon to help estimate a project's impact to existing content and to help provide a rough estimate for the amount of work and how long the project might take.

Since this phase is so different depending upon the environment, and since new or inexperienced content strategists don't usually have to participate in this phase, I won't cover it further in the book.

- **Discovery Phase** – This is the "let's all get acquainted and figure out what this project is all about" phase. In this phase, the team is assembled, and everyone reviews and asks questions about what was promised in the proposal. They would meet with the client or sponsor to get more details about the problem that they are trying to solve. At this point the biggest issue is trying to keep the client or sponsor from trying to design the finished product. This phase is for learning. A content strategist would learn as much as possible about what the clients/sponsors are currently doing, what content they have, and how it was produced.

- **Analysis Phase** - This is thinking time. Once the team has gathered a pile of information, they need some time to go back to the office and sort through it all. This phase usually results in a stack of deliverables that go back to the client. Some of these deliverables are project plans and cost estimates for the various ways the project might proceed. A content strategist would spend a good deal of time understanding the proposed solutions and figuring out the content work that needs to be done for each. The content strategist would also have a list of deliverables to deliver to the client providing analysis of various content issues.

- **Design Phase** – At this point the client/sponsor has decided upon an approach and the final solution is designed in detail. Everyone on the team is busy in this phase figuring out exactly how the project will be built. A content strategist would focus on what existing content will be re-purposed, what has to created from scratch, who is going to do the work, what the editorial processes will be, what are the editorial standards, and so on. This is a very busy time and there are a lot of decisions that must be made before the writing work can start.

- **Build Phase** – This is where the work gets done. The blueprints are done and now all that's left to do is to build the house. In this phase the content strategist will probably be writing some content, supervising others who are writing or repurposing content, editing content that is being developed by the client/sponsor, and reporting on progress and how well the team is keeping to the estimated budget.

- **Test Phase** – A website is not a book; it has a lot of moving parts and functionality that must be tested before it is ready to be turned over to the client/sponsor. The content needs to be tested and approved along with any functional portions of the site. During testing the content strategist would be responsible for providing the test team with guidance on what content work was done (what is new and what has changed) and a list of specific content changes that the testers should look for to verify that all the content work actually made it into the finished product. The content strategist would also develop a plan for dealing with defects found during testing.
- **Maintenance Phase** – As soon as a new website is launched, it is out of date. A content strategist would develop a plan for the creation of new content for the site, an editorial calendar for exactly what content might be created and when it will be needed to support planned business needs, and removal and archiving of old material on an ongoing basis.

Hopefully, it is becoming very clear now how a good Web content strategist can really add value, and become an important and vital member of the website development team.

# Chapter 2 – Why Web Development Project Plans

**Fail -** *And How Web Content Strategy Can Help*

I was originally going to call this chapter, "Why Most Web Development Project Plans Suck," and that seemed a little harsh—but only a little. So before we get into the details of building content, I want to touch on some issues around project planning and estimating work. If there is one place where an expert in the editorial process can add value to a project, this is it. Late projects are no fun for anyone and not having the content ready is one of the main causes of late projects.

Late content is **not** a minor aggravation. It is, according to many, the number one reason for late project delivery and negatively impacts the bottom line. How much does it cost an organization for every day that the Web development team is sitting idle waiting for content?

A thousand dollars? Ten thousand dollars? More? It's a lot, and it's also completely avoidable.

But avoiding this problem will require some different thinking about how your team plans the content track of your projects. Having a nice, pretty, detailed project plan is not going to solve this problem. In fact, project plans are generally the *cause* of the problem! I've seen this over and over again in "lessons learned" meetings after a project is finished. Someone asks, "so, why was the content late?" After much discussion and going around and around, the answer is usually that the content *did not arrive later than it should have.* There was not much anyone could have done to make it happen faster. What *was* wrong was how the content development process was estimated when the project plan was created. **It was an unreasonable project plan based on flawed assumptions**.

This flawed planning usually has one of the following three root causes:

- Arbitrary time frames
- Lack of understanding of editorial processes
- Failure to really plan for missed deadlines

## Arbitrary Time Frames

This means that the project planners didn't do all the work necessary to figure out exactly what content work needed to be done and how long it would take to do each piece. They just planned the content development around another time line such as technical development. Project planners often just ask the technical development team when they are going to need the content and work the project plan back from there without regard for reality.

It often happens like this:

- The project is set to officially start on April 1.
- The programmers tell the project planner that they will be ready to deal with the site content on June 1, two months later.
- The project planner enters a line in the project plan that says "Content Development April 1 thru June 1."

And that's as much thought as it gets.

Is it possible to do the content development for this project in 2 months? Maybe, but it needs a lot more thought and analysis than that. Eventually, someone has to figure out:

- How many pages need to be created or edited
- How many people are available to work on the content and how many hours a week do they have
- How long (roughly) will it take to create a new page and get it through all the editorial processes
- How long (roughly) will it take to make edits to an existing page and get it through all the editorial processes

Then it's just a matter of doing the math.
A very simple example might look like this:

> (**50 new pages** to be created) X (4 hours per page for writing, editing, and approvals) = **200 hours**

> (**200 existing product description pages** need to be reformatted and edited) X (2 hours per page for editing and approvals) = **400 hours**

> (Time needed for project ramp up, meetings, and testing) = **60 hours**

> **Total** Content Development Project Time = **660 hours**

Now you have some real data to work with. If you plan a full-time content person's work week at 35 hours, and you have 8 weeks allotted for content development, then one person would work 280 hours in 8 weeks. Since we now have a reasonable time estimate for the work of 660 hours, it becomes clear that you will probably need three people working full time for 8 weeks to do the content development. If you don't have three people, can't hire and train them by April, or can't start the content development work on April 1 for any other reason, then the project plan needs to be re-worked based on reality, not wishes and hopes.

# Lack of Understanding of the Editorial Process

Even when project planners do try to include more detail about content development into the plan, they often just don't know enough about all of the editorial processes, what is simple and what is complex, and in what order things need to be done to create an accurate plan. A content development expert needs to be consulted in order to give the plan real meaning. Content development is not a solitary act; it is an ongoing process that usually involves a lot of people. To make an accurate plan, you need to completely understand each process, who will be performing that process, how many times will they have to perform this process, and how long each iteration takes.

# Failure to Really Plan for Missed Deadlines

So you have a content milestone in the project plan. If you don't have an agreed-upon contingency plan for each milestone, you really don't have a plan. You can't wait until someone is late to figure out, "now what." For every deadline and milestone in the plan, you need to have a checkpoint at the 80 percent completion point and have an agreement on exactly what will happen if the task is not 80-percent complete. Everyone should know up front what will happen if deadlines are missed, you have buy-in from the project managers, and if it happens, you just do it and the project moves along on schedule.

Content approvals by subject matter experts are frequently late. When we are planning the project, I make sure to get these approvers to agree that they feel they have enough time allotted. I get them to commit to the dates we have planned. I set a checkpoint for them to judge how well they are doing. They must have 80 percent of the work completed when 80 percent of the time they have to complete the work has passed. If they do not have this amount of work done, I will bypass them and approve everything in their list myself. They will not have another chance to make content comments and suggest changes until the entire project goes into the testing phase. I make sure they also know that defects found in this phase of the process will be prioritized by severity and there is no guarantee that the changes will be made before the project launches unless they are classified as critical.

This is an example of having a clear backup plan for an important milestone. If these plans are made up front, and everyone agrees to what will happen if things are late, it's amazing how few deadlines are missed. And if they are missed, I don't have to have a series of panicked meetings to decide what to do. I just do what we decided up front and keep the project moving forward.

The Web Content Strategist's Bible

# Chapter 3 – Content Strategy During the Discovery Phase

Discovery is the initial phase of a Web development project. This includes the first meetings with the client/sponsor, discussions about what the client is looking for, identifying the problem or business issue to be solved, and learning about the client's business and organization. During Discovery, the Content Strategist needs to learn as much as possible about the client's current editorial assets, the size and experience level of any editorial staff, and content-related technical concerns.

If a project is particularly content-heavy, a Content Workshop may also be required. How to set up and run a Content Workshop is described later in this chapter.

During Discovery the content strategist needs to focus on learning about the content assets and processes that currently exist, and defining the requirements for a successful project. How the team will get there will be figured out later. Right now you need to focus on what you have as a starting point and where you want to end up when the journey is over.

Each phase of the development process builds on what you learned in the previous phase; so it is essential that when you are face to face with the client/sponsor you ask the right questions and document everything you learn so you and the team can refer back to it later when everyone is back in the office.

# Discovery Phase Documents/Deliverables

Here are the kinds of documents and client deliverables you might be asked to create during the Discovery Phase:

- Content Project Summary
- Content Inventory or Content Audit
- Content Datascape
- Missing Source Content Report
- Content Workshop Agenda
- Content Assumptions
- Content Requirements

## Content Project Summary Worksheet

Use this worksheet to start to gather important information about a project as soon as you are assigned. Make sure you gather all the information and ask the right questions when you are with the client/sponsor.

---

The Web Content Strategist's Bible

The Content Summary Worksheet should contain the following information:

*Table 1 – Content Project Summary Worksheet*

| Document Field | Description/Notes |
|---|---|
| Client Company Name | This could also be a department for internal projects. |
| Project Name | You may be working on several projects for the same client/sponsor, make sure you have an agreed upon title for the project. |
| Project Number | Capture any account or billing numbers associated with the project. |
| Primary Customer Contact | Name and contact information for the client/sponsor--office phone, mobile, email address, mailing address, and any other contact information you require. |
| Project Team Lead | Name and contact information for the leader/manager of your project team. The team usually has a project manager, lead consultant, or account executive. |
| Project manager | Name and contact information |
| Information Architect | Name and contact information |
| Technical Lead | Name and contact information |
| Creative Lead (art director etc.) | Name and contact information |

| Document Field | Description/Notes |
|---|---|
| Content Lead (list yourself) | Name and contact information |
| Other team members | Name and contact information |
| Current website URL | The URL of the page currently live on the Web. |
| Login ID and password | It is critical to get an ID and password that gives you access to all areas of the site. |
| Competitors website URLs | List all of the major industry competitors along with any needed IDs and passwords. |
| Project Description | Describe the project at a high level and reference any other documents (statements of work, contracts, etc.) that describe the project in detail. Include links to these documents if possible. |
| Project audience | Start to gather information about who will be consuming the content created for the project including demographic data and roles, responsibilities, level of technical/Web knowledge, and so on. |

The Web Content Strategist's Bible

| Document Field | Description/Notes |
|---|---|
| Propose content tasks | List the kinds of content related activities that will be required by the project. This could include:<br><br>• Creation of new content<br>• Repurposing of existing Web content<br>• Repurposing of content from some other media such as print<br>• Light editing of content to be created by others<br>• Proofreading only<br>• Inputting of existing content into a WCMS<br>• Scriptwriting for product demos |
| Quantity of proposed content | For each type listed above, get enough information to make a rough guess as to how many pages will be required or enough information to be able to estimate the amount of work involved. |
| Client/sponsor contact for content-related issues | Whenever possible, get a client contact who can answer content-specific questions. |
| Other subject matter experts (SMEs) | It's never too soon to start collecting contact information for all kinds of SMEs that might be needed for the project. |

This is a document that you will be referring back to for the entire project. As team members and SMEs change, keep this document up-to-date. If your team does not have another method for doing so, you can also use this document to store links to all other project related documents.

## Content Inventory Spreadsheet

The IA on the project normally does the content inventory; so, I'm not suggesting here that this be taken over by the content strategist entirely. In performing the content inventory, the IA not only learns about what content is on an existing site, but also how the site is structured and a lot about the business. It's an important job for an IA to perform.

But it is certainly not unheard of for a content strategist to help out with this very tedious activity to speed up the process. I also advocate letting the content strategist inventory all of the client's content that may not be on the existing website, but may be relevant.

For an existing website, a content inventory is created by starting on the home page, identifying all the major categories and then clicking through the site, page by page, and recording information about every single content item found. It can be quite a job.

If there is not an existing website, then it is a matter of finding all the relevant content, in whatever media, and recording the information. This could include brochures, catalogs, videos, training material, direct mail, multi-media

The Web Content Strategist's Bible

presentations, etc. Everything is fair game for the inventory list.

This information is gathered in a content inventory spreadsheet with each item having its own row and information filled in the each other the following column headings:

*Table 2 – Content Inventory Worksheet*

| Spreadsheet Column Heading | Description/Notes |
|---|---|
| Numerical identifier | For existing Web content, most IAs will use a numbered system to identify each content item. The homepage will be 1.0. The top categories will be 1.1, 1.2 etc. All the existing categories will be identified this way. This is not needed for content not currently in a website. |
| Description | The page title or document description |
| Link URL | Record for page on an existing site |
| Content type | This is usually the file format – HTML, PDF, Flash demo, Word .doc, Excel spreadsheet, video (mp4), etc. |
| Content function | What kind of content is it? Product description, index page, press release, executive |

| Spreadsheet Column Heading | Description/Notes |
|---|---|
| | bio, application help, email template, etc. |
| Content owner | Whose job it is to maintain this page. |
| Keywords | It's a good idea to start a list of keywords or topics associated with each piece of content found. At some point this should be reconciled with an official list of keywords and taxonomy. It helps if everyone calls things by the same name. |
| Update frequency | Is the content updated daily, monthly, rarely, or never? |
| Source content storage location | Where, exactly, does the source file for this item live? If it is only on someone's hard drive, make sure you list that. This is especially important for content that is not currently on the website. Just because a client has a printed catalog, for instance, does not mean that the digital source file used to create it can be located. It's nice to know up front which items might have to be re-created. This column usually has a disturbing number of entries labeled "unknown." |

| Spreadsheet Column Heading | Description/Notes |
|---|---|
| Current status | Mark this column if the content is obsolete, incorrect, or no longer timely. |
| Restricted access | If certain content can only be seen by certain users with a certain log-in profile, capture this as best you can. Or if certain offline content should not be viewed by anyone outside the company, make a note. |
| Notes | Anything else that might eventually be useful. |

# Existing Content Audit

Performing a comprehensive content inventory can be a long and time-consuming process for a larger site. A more cost-effective option might be to only perform a content audit as opposed to a complete content inventory.

A content audit is just a sampling of a small bit of the site's content to get a general idea about the kinds and volume of the content on the site. The idea is to gather a few examples of every type of content that is offered on the site. It's not necessary to examine every content item and page, but at least one of every major type.

A content audit spreadsheet similar to the one used for a content inventory. See the table below for the types of data to be collected and recorded in this spreadsheet.

## *Table 3 – Existing Content Audit Spreadsheet*

| Spreadsheet Column Heading | Description/Notes |
|---|---|
| Description | The page type or document type description |
| Example Link URL | Record a page URL of an existing page that serves as a good example of this type of content (product pages, press releases etc.) |
| Content file type | This is usually the file format – HTML, PDF, Flash demo, Word .doc, Excel spreadsheet, video (mp4), etc. |
| Content function | What kind of content is it? Product description, index page, press release, executive bio, application help, email template, etc. |
| Content Volume | Approximately how many pages of this type are on the site? |
| Keywords | It's a good idea to start a list of keywords or topics associated with each piece of content found. At some point this should be reconciled with an official list of keywords and taxonomy. It helps if everyone refers to the different parts of the site by the same name. |

## Content Datascape

This is really just another way of looking at the content inventory once it is finished. The idea is to re-sort the spreadsheet so you can see all of the various places where content is stored and which items of content are stored in which locations.

It is essential that you be very thorough when gathering this data. It is not enough to note that the content is stored in a database. You need to list where the database is hosted and how to get into the contents. I was on a project once where we learned during this step that most of the content we needed for an online catalog lived inside a proprietary database that only a handful of programmers knew how to access, and they were all booked up for the next year and had no time to write code to give our project access. The sooner these issues are found and resolved, the better.

## Missing Source Content Report

This is something I usually provide back to the client/sponsor as a courtesy and a heads-up.

This is simply a listing of all the content for which we were not able to locate any digital source content file. I list the items by priority with the top items being things we know we want to use in the project that will have to be manually recreated if the source file is not found. This gives the client a chance to look around for the files and, if necessary, go ahead and have them recreated in digital format.

## Content Workshop Agenda

For content-heavy projects, or projects that require the input and agreement of many players, it is a good idea to get everyone in a room at once and talk through any content issues you may have to gain a consensus. This is especially true if there are many people who will need to sign off on the final product. Now is the time to uncover differences of opinion, not after everything is written, edited, approved, and translated.

Every content workshop is different. The goal is to get answers to content-related questions so agenda items will vary. Here are some common topics covered in most content workshops:

*Table 4 – Content Workshop Agenda*

| Agenda Item | Description |
|---|---|
| Introductions and explanations of roles | Most people who do not work in Web development have no idea what an IA or a content strategist is or does. This is a good time to explain areas of responsibility. |
| Brief description of project impact to Web content | Focus specifically on the content impacts of the project. What is new? What will |

| Agenda Item | Description |
|---|---|
| | change? What will go away? What will be completely re-written? What will be accomplished if the changes are successful? |
| Brand voice presentation | Many large companies have someone specifically in charge of the company's branding. Ask the branding specialist to come and present an idea of how the brand should be represented in the project's content.<br><br>If the client/sponsor does not have defined brand guidelines, then lead a discussion to create a list of adjectives that describe how the client would like the content to be perceived by a reader:<br><br>• Professional<br>• Friendly<br>• Smart<br>• Edgy<br>• Conservative<br>• Etc. |

| Agenda Item | Description |
|---|---|
| Voice and tone discussion | Now that you understand the overall brand representation, talk with the group about what the voice and tone of the content should be.

Do this for each different section of the project to see if the voice and tone changes. Product specifications pages may need to be terse and technical, whereas product marketing pages may need to focus more on the positive feelings associated with using the product instead of a list of features. |
| Content-specific requirements discussion | Go through the defined project requirements, and talk about any requirements that are content-specific or have large content impacts to gather more details that might not be listed.

For instance, exactly what languages are to be supported on the site. Just listing "Spanish" is too vague. What version of Spanish? Mexican Spanish is different from Puerto |

| Agenda Item | Description |
|---|---|
| | Rican Spanish and both are very different from Castilian Spanish spoken in Spain. The same goes for Canadian French and French spoken in France. How will Queen's English be handled? Will everything be authored in American English?<br><br>Do they have existing content that they think can be reused without editing? Does everyone agree? |
| Editorial style guide discussion | Find out if there is an existing style guide for writing or if the authors should go by AP, Chicago, etc. Ask if the client has a list of how it prefers to use Web-specific terms such as email, e-mail, or E-mail. If not, talk about a process for deciding on these editorial issues as they come up. |

# Chapter 4 – Content Strategy During the Analysis Phase

At some point in the project, your team will be asked to collect everything they have learned and make sense out of it all. Often this analysis is the most important thing that the client/sponsor is paying you for. Your team has the expertise that this project requires, and here is where you will be asked to analyze what they have and what they want, then make recommendations. This is the Analysis phase.

The content strategist's job during this phase is to make recommendations to the clients/sponsors about how the content track of this project should proceed based on what you have learned about their current content practices and your content development expertise.

There is really only one major content strategy deliverable in this phase, and that is the Content Strategy Document (actually a bundling of many smaller documents).

# The Content Strategy Document

The Content Strategy document is a compilation of a number of analysis documents. Exactly which documents to include will vary per project depending on the project's requirements. An IA may do some of this analysis, and some of the analysis may not be needed at all. But this document is the vehicle for communicating what you have learned about the project and the client/sponsor. Further, you will use this document to make specific recommendations about how you think the content track of the project should proceed. Not all of your ideas will be implemented, but you are being paid for your expertise; so don't be shy about making suggestions. This frequently becomes part of an even larger deliverable to the client that contains analysis and recommendations from all the team members.

Possible subsections of this document include:
- Existing Content Analysis
- Content Gap Analysis of Current Site
- Competitive Content Analysis
- Editorial Process Analysis
- Readiness Analysis

## *Existing Content Analysis*

This is your chance to give the clients/sponsors an objective, outside look at their current Web content. If there is a chance that content currently used in some other medium is planned for use on the Web as part of this project, then mention that content in the analysis as well. Here are the topics to cover in your analysis.

*Table 5 – Existing Content Analysis Report*

| Item | Description |
|------|-------------|
| Readability | The analysis is divided into several sub categories. |

| Item | Description |
|------|-------------|
| • Scanability | Very few users approach unfamiliar text on the Web by reading word-for-word from the top to the bottom. They scan, looking quickly through the text for information relevant to the task at hand. Users have described long blocks of undivided text during research testing as boring, intimidating, and just too much trouble.<br><br>Analyze the current content for appropriate and consistent use of structures and formats that help scannability such as:<br>• Page Titles<br>• Headings<br>• Large type<br>• Bold text<br>• Highlighted text<br>• Bulleted lists<br>• Captions for graphics<br>• Topic sentences<br>• Tables of contents and indexes<br><br>If you find pages with scannability issues, include examples. |

| Item | Description |
|------|-------------|
| • Conciseness | The preference for concise, to-the-point information on the Web has been established by research (Morkes and Nielsen, 1997). Compounding the need for compact information display is the finding that users read about twenty-five percent slower online. Evaluate the content for conciseness and show examples of long wordy pages if found. |
| • Objectivity | Online readers have an automatic and strongly negative response to an overly promotional writing style. Anything resembling "marketese" or self-serving hyperbole is immediately discounted and detracts from the user's trust of the information presented. Examine the content for unsupported claims that use words like "best," "fastest," "strongest," etc. When you find these statements, ask |

| Item | Description |
|---|---|
| | the simple question: "Says who?" |
| Effectiveness of communicating the brand message | Hopefully, a list of brand attributes has been established by this point in the project. Review the existing content to see how well the current content communicates these attributes. |
| | Does the content do a good job of explaining "who you are," "what you believe," and "why the customer should put faith in your products and services"? The website content must reinforce the equity and promise of the brand. |
| Recommendations | Based on your analysis, make some clear recommendations about what could be done to make the existing content better serve the client/sponsor. |
| | A very effective tool to use is to make a Before and After mock-up of how an |

| Item | Description |
|------|-------------|
|      | existing page would look if the suggested changes were made. Improvements in scannability are immediately noticeable when the client can see pages side by side where the only thing that has changed is how the text is structured. |

See Appendix A of this book for more information on research that backs up these suggested changes.

## *Content Gap Analysis of Current Site*

If you are working with an IA, the IA will almost always perform a Gap Analysis against competitors and similar websites. The goal of this analysis is to find out what features and content areas are already being provided by some of your competitors, and to figure out which basic site features and content areas are being offered by *all* of your competitors. The features being offered by all competitors are then considered basic "must haves" for the site if you want even be in the same league as the other sites offering a similar product or service.

At its most basic level, the structure is a simple spreadsheet similar to the following example:

## Table 6 – Content Gap Analysis Spreadsheet

| Feature / Content area | Current URL | Competitor 1 URL | Competitor 2 URL | Notes | Grade (A - F) |
|---|---|---|---|---|---|
| Search | http://www... | http://www ... | http://www ... | Comp 1 has advanced search and saved searches that we and comp 2 do not. | B |
| Executi ve Bios | Missing | http://www ... | http://www ... | Both Comp 1 and Comp 2 have biographic al data on the executive team. We do not currently have this on the site. | F |
| Product finder | http://www... | Missing | Missing | Our guided product finder application has not been adopted yet by our competitor s. | A+ |

Don't mistake this for oversimplifying the gap analysis process. Entire consulting engagements consist of nothing more than doing this analysis on a very detailed basis for very large and complicated websites. This is not something that a content strategist would be called upon to do often. But a customer might want a basic gap analysis and not have an IA available or be able to afford an IA.

## *Competitive Content Analysis*

A Competitive Content Analysis takes a deeper dive into content on competitors' sites than a gap analysis generally does. This analysis is usually done for a subset of all the content types on the site that have been identified as critical to the project's success. It might not make sense to compare two company's press releases for content differences, but it makes a lot of sense to see exactly how a competitor is describing products and services.

The report itself is created in a spreadsheet similar to the gap analysis document. A partial example might look like this:

## Table 7 – Competitive Content Analysis Spreadsheet

| Type of Page | Our Content | Comp 1 | Comp 2 | Analysis |
|---|---|---|---|---|
| Product | Currently we have a static page listing feature, benefits, and technical Specs. Written in a professional, but unemotional style. We have one product image. | They have similar product descriptions but have images that can be zoomed and viewed from different angles. | They push the technical product specs to a different page and write the product descriptions with more emotion emphasizing how much fun it is to use the product. | Comp 2 has a best-in–class implementation that we should consider emulating and for certain, high-margin products, adding some kind of rich media presentation as well. |

Specific recommendations or directions should be expanded upon outside of the spreadsheet. If ten or more content areas are analyzed, highlight the most important two or three in the text of the document outside the spreadsheet as well.

## *Editorial Process Analysis*

The purpose of the Editorial Process Analysis document is to discover and document the process that the client/sponsor currently uses to publish Web content, and to make recommendations about what the process should be for this project. If there is no current website, you can modify this to cover how they create printed material. If you have been writing for any length of time, you probably know more about this process than you think. Most of it is just common sense, but for many companies, their website is the only thing they publish so they may not be editorial experts.

A good Editorial Process Analysis document should provide answers to the following questions:

- Where do requests for new or updated content originate?
- Is there a dedicated content staff?
- Who assigns the work?
- Who performs the work?
- Who edits or proofs the work?

- Who is responsible for creating and updating graphics and images?
- Who is responsible for creating and updating an internal editorial style guide (if they have one).
- Who has to approve the work's factual content?
- Is there a legal approval?
- Is there a single, final approver such as a managing editor?
- Is the content creation and editing process handled in one central location, or can people in various locations make changes? Are any of these people outside the country?
- Do all content changes go through the same approval process or does it change depending upon the kind of content?
- Who decides who gets to approve or reject content changes?
- Are there testing and staging environments (servers) where authors of digital content can view their changes in context?
- How is work routed from author to approver etc.? Is there an automated workflow system, is everything is just sent by email, or is everything printed out and routed physically?
- Once the content is approved, how does the Web page get created? Are there programmers who code HTML or the content authors have tools to generate the page code?
- What is their established process for removing old or unneeded content from the production servers?

- Is there a WCMS? If so, get the details on where the company got it, how long it has been in use, is it being used in a standard, off-the-shelf configuration or has it been heavily customized? If so, who did the custom programming? Did the client use their own programming team or a consultant?
- Once new content is approved, how does it get onto the live website production servers? Is this handled by the WCMS or does someone have to manually copy the files to the server?
- Are there restrictions on when or how often new content files can be published to the production servers?
- Is there an editorial calendar that lists planned content changes for the next 6 months or so?
- Are there parts of the site that get regularly scheduled updates every day, week, month, etc.?
- Is there a separate process for handling emergency updates to the website? If so, what is the process and who is involved?
- Are there other planned content changes scheduled to occur while the current project is running? If so, who will be responsible for coordinating the changes? What safeguards are in place to prevent multiple groups from trying to make changes to the same content?
- Is any content on the current website being translated? If so, what process is used for translations?

- Does the client perform the translations in-house or send the content out to a vendor? How is all of this tracked? If the client uses a vendor, how much advance notice does the vendor need to prepare for new translations?
- Once the translations are complete, does someone else verify the translations before they are published or do they just trust that what the vendor has provided is accurate and appropriate?
- Are there backup, archiving, or other content governance policies that must be followed?
- Is there content on the site that must match certain printed material? If so, who handles this coordination?
- During testing, is there a tool or system used to log and track defects? How is this process handled?

Use these questions to analyze and document the client's current editorial process. Use examples as needed to highlight process strengths and weaknesses.

## Making Editorial Process Recommendations

As you go through your analysis, you will likely find some processes that are missing altogether, and some processes that have significant holes in them. Here is your chance to define all the process issues and make specific recommendations about how content will be handled for your current project.

It is a good idea to use as much of the client's existing editorial process as you can when planning your project. There is no need to re-create an existing, functioning process, but it would be nice to know up front that the process has certain known limitations. For example, many technical teams set aside one day a week for server maintenance and no new files can be uploaded that day. Make sure that you understand the limitations of the existing system so you can plan around them.

It is also important to make sure that you are in line with what others on your team are proposing. If part of the project is to implement a Web content management system, then you should make sure that your proposed editorial process reflects this system.

Your proposal for defining an editorial process to be used for the current project should answer most of the questions listed above. Make sure you understand who has to approve what kinds of content, how the work is going to flow from one person to another, and how it is all going to be tracked.

## Readiness Analysis

How ready is the project team and the client/sponsor to do the content work needed for the project to be a success? You need to evaluate and document the level of readiness in three areas: resource readiness, process readiness, and technology readiness.

## Content Resource Readiness

- Are there enough people to do the work in the time allotted in the project plan?
- Does the current content staff have the necessary skills needed for the project?
- Can additional full-time or contracting staff be hired?
- Is the planned content staffing budget sufficient?
- Who has the responsibility of hiring additional staff, the project team or the client/sponsor?
- Is there enough time before the project is scheduled to start to hire and train additional resources?
- Is there someone with enough time who can train and supervise additional people?
- Is there enough physical workspace for more people?
- Are there computers available for additional people, or budget to buy or lease them?
- Will additional software licenses need to be purchased (WCMS, etc.) and are they budgeted for?
- Will all the various subject matter experts and content approvers be available when needed?

## Content Process Readiness

- List any missing processes found during the editorial process analysis here.
- List any processes with significant holes or missing steps here.
- List any new processes that need to be created.

- List any new people or departments who are expected to participating in these new processes. For example, if it has been determined that a legal review will be needed as part of the content approval process for this project, has the legal department agreed to participate and free up the necessary resources?

## Content Supporting Technologies Readiness

- Describe the WCMS readiness. Will any programming work need to be done on an existing WCMS to prepare for this project? Can this work be completed and tested by the time the authors need to start entering content into the WCMS? **Note**: This is a huge dependency that is often missed during project planning. If there are WCMS changes that need to be made to support content creation, make sure that everyone understands that your content development work cannot start until the WCMS work is completed, tested, debugged, and formally accepted.
- Describe any defect and issue tracking software used during the content development process? If this software will be used, is it ready, or is there a firm plan to have it ready by the time that content development begins?
- Describe the readiness of any other technical systems that might be needed during the content development process.

The Web Content Strategist's Bible

# Chapter 5 – Content Strategy During the Design Phase

In the Design Phase, it is time to stop talking about what you *could* do, or *might* do, and to create a design for exactly what your team is actually *going* to do. Your goal as a content strategist at this point in the project is to figure out exactly what content needs to be modified or created, and figure out exactly how the work is going to be done. This is the time to define all of the processes and handoffs so that when the writers are ready to start creating content they can concentrate on what they are doing, not how they are going to do it.

During the Design Phase, the content strategist wears a lot of hats. He or she works with the graphics designers and art directors to get a feel for what they are doing and give editorial input to text placement and names if needed. He or she may also work with the technical team to help design the content management system input templates that writers will use to create new content. It may also be necessary to design new processes for the creation, approval, and technical implementation of editorial content, depending upon what currently exists.

But the most time-consuming tasks for a content strategist during the Design Phase are:

- Building the content matrix
- Creating an editorial style guide that is to be used by those who will be doing the actual writing for the site
- Defining the content approval process
- Consulting on WCMS development needs

## The Content Matrix

Of all the documents described in this book, this is the most important. The Content Matrix will be your guide and tracking tool as the project moves into the Build Phase. The more complete and up-to-date your content matrix is, the easier things will go once you start developing content.

This document is so important that when I am interviewing job candidates if I see the words "content matrix" on their resume or they mention the term in conversation, I am very interested in them as it shows that they understand the importance of clearly identifying every content item and tracking the work to be performed.

The idea of the content matrix is simple—create a spreadsheet that captures all the attributes and delivery milestones for each and every little piece of content that has to be touched in any way for the project. Actually building one is a very complex process and keeping it up-to-date is a chore, but the idea is easy. Every bit of content on the site that needs to be created, edited, or reviewed needs to be captured and tracked.

If there is some content that the IAs are responsible for, such as field labels or navigational labels, then these items are not usually listed in the matrix. The same goes for text that may be used on a screen that is part of an online application if this text is tracked in some other way, such as wire frame documents.

## *Building a Content Matrix*

A content matrix is almost always a spreadsheet. How you actually construct it will depend upon how familiar you are with using spreadsheets and the complexity of the information you are gathering. Basically, you will create a column for each attribute or date you want to capture then create rows of each content item to be tracked. If the project is large and complex, you might also want to further subdivide the information using worksheets or tabs. Take a look at Figure 1 later in the chapter to see how the following columns and color suggestions might be used.

## Content Matrix Rows

Use documents created by the IA as a good starting point for identifying the individual items that need to go into the content matrix as rows. The IAs will normally create the document that defines the site structure and a site map as part of the design process. Keep in mind, however, that these documents may not list every page on the proposed website. They may stop at large categories such as "Product Pages." Remember that the content team may have to create every single instance in the product page category (one page for every individual product); so each instance needs to be captured and tracked in the content matrix. If the website plans to show a product page for 100 products, and the content team has to create, edit, or modify these pages in any way (even if they are stored in a database and not as HTML), then you will need to have 100 product rows in your matrix. It is easy to see how this can get to be a very large spreadsheet.

Also, if you will be creating content using a Web Content Management System that stores content in reusable modules, then you may also have to subdivide pages into the modules used to create that page and capture every module in the content matrix.

An example of this situation might be a product page that had three major headings—Features, Benefits, and Guarantee. The Features section would be different for each product. The Benefits section might be the same for several products in the same category and the Guarantee section might be exactly the same for every product. So the text for each of these headings would be captured in its own module so that it can be reused. This way, if the terms of the Guarantee change, the change only has to be made in one place, not on every product page. So for this kind of structure, you would need a row in the content matrix for the page and a row showing every module that is used to construct that page.

Another good tool to use when working on rows in your content matrix is color. You might use a different background for rows listing pages, or you might change the color of the first cell in the row to indicate its current status such as:

- Green = complete
- Yellow = out for review
- Red = unresolved issue

This is just one idea. Color can be used in lots of ways to help you identify kinds of content quickly or scan for content items with problems. Just be sure to define your color use in a legend somewhere on the matrix so the next person to use it will understand what all the colors mean.

## Content Matrix Columns

Columns should be created in your matrix to capture information that a content author would need to know, or to capture the date when work is due or completed. Anyone involved in the project should be able to look at the content matrix and understand the current state of any content line item.

Your columns should follow a logical order from left to right. Start on the left with basic, general information and place more specific information further to the right. Try to list columns in the order in which the information will be needed. The same thing holds true for dates. Set the columns to capture dates in order from left to right.

Ideally, you should be able to hand a portion of the content matrix to a content author and, with a little explanation, the author would have all the information required to do the work defined in that part of the matrix.

## Column Headings

The exact columns needed for a matrix will change depending upon the project and what you need to capture. Here are some possible column types with explanations to give you an idea what to think about:

**Page?** – Is this a page or a module in the WCMS? If the content is being created as either a page or a module on a page, capture this information here. You can use this column for sorting. Sometimes you just want to view the rows with pages in your spreadsheet. Having the rows marked as either Page or Module will let you hide one or the other as needed.

**Asset ID/File name and location** – Within the Content Management System, every file (Page or Module) has a unique identifier. The IAs usually create the naming standards. If a WCMS is not being used, then capture the file name and location of the working version of the document. If someone else had to work on that particular piece of content, how would the author find it? List the complete file name and include hard drive identifier (for example,

The Web Content Strategist's Bible

O:documents/project33/products/loafers.html).

**Page/Module Description** – If the item is a page, this is the page title. If it is a module, this is a short description of what is in the module.

**Content/Page Type** – If this content item is stored in a WCSM, list the template name used to create it. In the WCMS content is created content using templates, and these templates are usually referred to as Content Types. If a WCMS is not used, list the page function or category (Product page, Press Release, etc.).

**Website area/category** – Used for Pages only, this column captures the main place in the site where the page will appear. Refer to the IA documents for this information. For example, this could be Shopping, or About Us.

**URL (pages only)** – For pages only, this is the complete URL and HTML file name to be generated or created for the finished page (http://xxxx.html).

**Existing URL (Current)** – If this is a page that currently exists in the system, list the complete URL here so you can click to go see the page in production out on the Web.

**Affected by this Project?** – Often you will be working with an existing content matrix that may include everything in the entire site or site area. Use this column to enter a "yes" if this item has to be touched in any way for this project. You can then sort to hide all of the unaffected content to have a much more manageable content matrix.

**Information Providers** – Who will be providing input to create and edit the content?

**Source Content Reviewers** – Who will be listed as part of the editorial workflow for content approval? Who will verify that the content is correct and accurate? If all the content has the same reviewers, or if there are several different lists of reviewers depending upon the content type, you can just indicate **List1** or **List2** in the field and list the actual names elsewhere in the document.

**Legal Reviewer** – If a legal review is required, list the reviewer's name in this field.

**Content Page/Module New?** – Is this a brand new page or module? Use this column for sorting to easily find new content.

**Description of Change** – What is going to change in the content? If the content already exists, the information in this column tells the author exactly what is to be changed. If this is new content, just list "Create New." This information can also be used later for testing if another person or another department is tasked with testing/verifying all your changes.

**Currently Used Internationally for which Countries/Languages?** – If this is existing content, list the countries or languages (depending upon which is appropriate) for which the content is tagged.

**New Countries/Languages** – If new countries or languages are being added, list them here.

**Word Count** – At some point in the project plan, you will be asked to provide a total count of words that will need to be translated, so record what has changed per Asset ID.

**Translation Instructions** – There are various ways to get content translated. You can send it out to a vendor, you can get someone internally to translate, or maybe you already have the translation. Include a description of this process in this column of the matrix.

**Author/Editor** – This job may be assigned to you, but sometimes you will assign work to others as part of your job. Use this field to track who is working on each piece of content.

**Content Complete** – This is a date field. When the author/editor is finished writing or editing a particular module, list the date here. You may also add a color to the cell (green) to indicate progress at a glance.

**Submitted for SME Review** – This is a date field, listing when the content was submitted for review, using whatever workflow process has been defined.

**SME/Reviewer Comments** – If a reviewer rejects a content module, list the needed change here so you can track it and verify the change later.

**Changes Made and Submitted Again** – Once suggested changes are made and the content is re-submitted for a second review, list the date here, and color code.

The Web Content Strategist's Bible

**SME Approval** – Once all SME reviewers have approved the content item, list the date here.

**Legal Approvals** – If legal approvals are done separately from the SME review listed above, use the same fields to capture this information.

**ME Approval Submitted** – If there is a final approver, such as a managing editor or project leader, capture the date that the content is submitted here.

**Translation Queue Verified** – After the content is approved, any content that has to go out for translation is usually captured on a translation list. A smart content strategist will check this list to verify that all the content items expected to be there are listed. Finding out late that a piece of content was never sent out for translation can really cause a last-minute scramble. Once this step is done, capture the date.

**Sent out for Translation** – Capture the date when the content is actually sent out for translation in this column.

**Translation Back from Vendor** – Capture the date that the content comes back from the translation vendor.

**Generate Page** – Once all of the edits have been approved, and translations are back from the vendor, there is often a step in the process to generate the page HTML code for each language and country. Capture the date that this is done.

**Generation Errors** – Capture any errors that are returned when the content is generated/published.

**URL for Internal Testing** – After the pages are generated they should go to an internal testing environment (used for content authors only), that mirrors the live site. The URL may be slightly different than the one used for production so capture that test site URL here.

**Verified in Internal Testing** – Record the date that you verified that the content item is checked and approved in this test environment.

**URL for User Acceptance Testing** – Once pages have passed internal testing, they are usually migrated to a complete test environment for everyone involved in the project to access and test. Capture that URL here.

**Verified in User Acceptance Testing** – Capture the date that you verified that the content item is good in this test environment.

**QA Approved** – If there is also a formal QA testing process that happens (should the client have a QA department that must sign off), enter the date here once this is complete.

**URL for Verification in Staging Environment** – Once that pages have passed internal and QA and testing, they are usually migrated to a staging environment that is exactly like the production environment. The technical team needs to make sure that nothing bad happens to the live site once this new content is uploaded. Include that URL here.

**Verified in Staging** – Capture the date that you verified that the content item is good in this test environment.

**Notes** – As problems or issues come up regarding a piece of content, capture them here.

These are not the only possible columns for a content matrix, but hopefully you get the idea of what should be captured and tracked. You need to be able to report on the status of any content item in the project at any time. The best way to do this is to have a complete and up-to-date content matrix. It can be as complex as you like. Maybe you want to link to other documents that define changes or edits. As long as you are comfortable with the document, go ahead.

Back up early and often! This is true for all documents, but it is critical for the content matrix. It may take a month to create, so you do not want to have to do that work twice!

**Shooogle Inc. Project - Content Matrix**

Version 0.8 - July 22, 2007

| Page or Module | CMS ID | Description | CMS Template | File Name | Conte Autho |
|---|---|---|---|---|---|
| **About Us** Section | | | | | |
| Page | about_exec_index | Executives Index Page | index_links | about/execs/index.html | L. Smit |
| Module | exec_links | list of execs | link_list | | L. Smit |
| Page | execs_griffith_bio_page | T.H. Griffith Biography page | bio_page | about/execs/griffith.htn | S. Dalla |
| Module | execs_griffith_bio | bio text | default_text | | S. Dalla |
| Module | execs_griffith_pic | photo - griffith | media_display | | S. Dalla |
| Module | execs_griffith_speech | speeches links griffith | link_list | | S. Dalla |
| Page | execs_cho_bio_page | M. Cho Biography page | bio_page | about/execs/cho.html | S. Dalla |
| Module | execs_cho_bio | bio text | default_text | | S. Dalla |
| Module | execs_cho_pic | photo - cho | media_display | | S. Dalla |
| Module | execs_cho_speech | speeches link cho | link_list | | S. Dalla |
| Page | about_hist_index | Company History Index | index_links | about_history.html | L. Smit |
| Module | hist_summary | summary of company history | default_text | | L. Smit |
| Module | building_pic_now | photo of current Shooogle building | media_display | | L. Smit |
| Module | building_pic_first | photo of first Shooogle location | media_display | | L. Smit |
| Page | hist_1996-2001_page | Early History | wide_page | about/hist/1996-2001.h | C. King |
| module | hist_1996-2001_text | early history text | default_text | | C. King |
| module | hist_1996-2001_pic | early history photo | media_display | | C. King |
| Page | hist_2002-2007_page | Recent History | wide_page | about/hist/2002-2007.h | C. King |
| module | hist_2002-2007_text | Recent history text | default_text | | C. King |
| module | hist_2002-2007_pic | Recent history photo | media_display | | C. King |

*Figure 1 – Content Matrix Example*

The Web Content Strategist's Bible

# Editorial Style Guide

An Editorial Style Guide for the project should be developed as a starting place for the creation of an official in-house editorial style guide to be used and maintained by the client.  Its function is to guide those with Web writing and editing responsibilities.

The goals of this guide are to:

- Promote consistency in the usage of technology and new media terms
- Set standards for grammatical usage
- Identify and explain common errors in grammar and word usage
- Specify certain formatting rules
- Clarify identification and usage of trademarked terms
- Act as a forum for the discussion, and continued re-evaluation, of changing conventions and the introduction of new terms and concepts

If the client/sponsor does not have some sort of style guide, at least a very basic document should be created that can become a record of decisions as conflicting issues arise and are resolved. If more than one or two people are going to be working on content for the project (including IAs and graphic designers), consistency will become a big problem without a style guide.

I once sat in an oak-paneled conference room at a Fortune 500 client while two managers almost came to blows over whether or nor to include a hyphen in the term "e-mail." I finally convinced them to use the hyphen, and all the editorial content was consistently written. But the graphic designer was never notified of the standard and delivered all the graphic banners and buttons without the hyphen. Document all these decisions and let everyone know. Don't learn the lesson the hard way like I did.

## *Sample Style Guide Table of Contents*

*Table 8 – Sample Style Guide Table of Contents*

| Document Section | Notes |
|---|---|
| **About This Guide** | |
| How This Guide Was Created | Include some notes about who created the guide, and how it can be updated and maintained. |
| Official Reference Guides | If other style guides such as AP, or The Chicago Manual of Style are also used, list them here along with the version number. Also list which guide takes precedence in the case of conflicts. |
| **Hyphenation and Compound Words** | |
| Hyphenated Titles - Capitalization | |
| Words Specific to this | This is a good place to |

| Document Section | Notes |
|---|---|
| Industry | capture business or industry-specific terms and how they will be used or avoided. |
| Prefixes | |
| Suffixes | |
| **Rules for Web Terminology** | |
| Company-specific Terms | This is a good place to capture company or client-specific terms and how they will be used or avoided. |
| Common Web/Internet Terms | There are many Web/Internet terms that do not yet have agreed upon rules. E-mail or email? Website, website, or Web site? Get an agreement among team members as to how these terms will be used for the project and enforce consistency. |
| **Acronyms/Abbreviations** | |
| i.e., e.g., and etc. | |
| State names | |
| Capitalization | |
| Commonly Used Acronyms | |

| Document Section | Notes |
| --- | --- |
| Other Acronym Information | |
| File Format Usage | |
| **Copyright Issues** | |
| Confidentiality Statements | |
| Referring to the Company | |
| Other Company Names and Products | Don't forget to define international usage here. |
| Use of ™ and ® | |
| **Punctuation and Capitalization** | Use these sections as necessary to describe perceived problem areas or places where the client/sponsor wants non-standard usage. |
| Period | |
| Comma | |
| Dash | |
| Ellipsis | |
| Colon | |
| Parentheses | |
| Capitalization of Items in a Series | |
| Capitalization of Articles, Prepositions, and Conjunctions | |

The Web Content Strategist's Bible

| Document Section | Notes |
|---|---|
| Capitalization of Titles | |
| Capitalization of Field Names and Link Text | This element is very important for IAs, graphic designers, and programmers. |
| **Numbers and Numerals** | |
| When to Spell out Numbers | |
| When to use Numerals | |
| Plural/Possessive Numbers | |
| Format for Phone Numbers | 1-800-555-1111 or 1(800) 555-1111. Also remember international phone numbers. |
| Format for Currency | Remember international usage. |
| **Problem Words and Phrases** | Include a few reminders about common problems and phrases. |
| Back up vs. Backup | |
| Disk vs. Disc | |
| Foreign Words | |
| Who vs. That | |
| That vs. Which | |
| Affect and Effect | |
| All vs. All of | |

| Document Section | Notes |
|---|---|
| Can vs. May | |
| OK vs. Okay | |
| Set up vs. Set-up | |
| **Formatting Issues** | |
| Fonts | |
| Endnote vs. Footnote Usage | |
| Paragraph Indents | |
| Referring to the Web | |
| Figure Captions and Table Titles | |
| Text References to Figures/Tables | |
| Headers and Footers | |
| Use of Small Caps | |
| **Trademarks** | |
| If there is a list of trademarked terms, include it here. Or include a link to a list maintained by the legal or brand departments. | |

| Document Section | Notes |
|---|---|
| **Standard Proofreading Marks** | If any proofing is going to be done on hardcopy, it is always a good idea to include a listing of proofreaders' marks, as many writers are no longer familiar with them. |
| **Index** | |

# Approval Process

The content for most Web projects will require some sort of approval before it can be posted live to the Web. Even within the same project, one kind of content may require the approval of four experts and the legal department, and another only has to be reviewed by someone in marketing and it's good to go. An Approval Process document describes the approval process to be used for the project and would answer these questions:

- **What has to be approved by whom?** – When the content authors get ready to start the content development process, they will need to know exactly how to route each piece of content. This document must specify which types of content have to go through what kind of approval, and then name the exact people responsible for the approvals. This is usually a set of lists, Content type A gets approved by all the people on List 1, Content type B gets approved by all the people on List 2, etc. If everything is to be approved by the same person or group, then this is easily documented.

- **What is the process for each kind of content?** - Once you know what kinds of content have to be approved and who the approvers are, you then need to establish and document the entire process. Some of the decisions you have to make may be dictated by the time you have in which to complete the project. Some things to consider are:
  - Who starts the process?

- o  Does everyone review the content at once?
     If so, you need to plan for reconciling
     conflicting comments.
- o  How many review/fix cycles will there be for
     each review? Typically the content is
     submitted for review, changes are
     requested, the author makes the agreed-
     upon changes, and the content is
     resubmitted for review. If there are further
     changes requested in this second review, the
     author will make them but not send the
     content back out for approval again.

A Process Diagram is the best way to show the
entire process with all the decisions that need to be made
along the way. Don't over-estimate your ability to describe
this process with words. Most people will need to see it
drawn out before they completely understand the flow.
Whenever it is possible and appropriate, use people's
names in the diagram. Few things get someone's attention
quicker than seeing their name in a diagram associated
with work to be done. See Figure 2 as an example of a
process flow diagram.

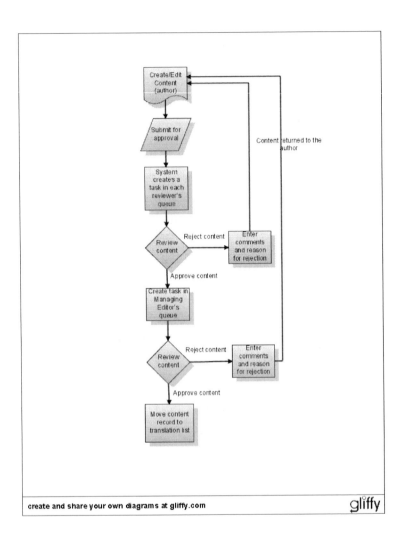

Figure 2 – Approval Process Diagram Example

The Web Content Strategist's Bible

# Translation Process

Translations will be covered in detail in another chapter, but establishing the process is definitely something that should be done during the Design Phase if you have content that will need to be translated. The tools you are using and the vendor may define a good bit of the process, but any good translation process should have these actions covered:

- **Translation Word Count Estimate** – Early in the project, an estimated translation word count needs to be made to get a rough idea of how many words will need to be translated for which languages. This estimate will be used by the team and the vendor to make sure that the proper resources are available when needed. This information will also let the vendor know how long the translations will take so this timeline can be added to the project plan. Most translation vendors have a maximum number of words per day that they can commit to translating.
- **Translation Schedule** – Based on the estimates, a schedule needs to be developed, listing when the vendor or translation resource can expect to receive the content for translation. These dates then need to be worked into the overall content project plan.
- **Specifying Languages** – This is the identification of which pieces of content need to be translated into which languages. This may be

handled with metadata if a WCMS is being used, or manually maintained in a spreadsheet.

- **Specifying Workflow** – There may be more than one method used for getting content translated. Maybe large bundles of content go out to an external translation vendor, and small changes are handled internally with a manual process. The content author needs a way to select which workflow is to be used for each piece of content.
- **Translation List Verification** – Before anything gets sent out to a vendor for translation, there should be a verification step in the process that lets all the authors check to make sure that the content assets they are responsible for are actually on the list.
- **Translation Tracking** – There should be a way to track exactly which assets are still out for translation, and which ones have been returned.
- **Translation Reviews** – Although translation vendors are very good at what they do, they are not experts in your client's company and customers. It is always a good idea to have someone within the company verify the translations.

Translations add a great deal of time and complexity to a project. That's why it is a common practice to launch a project initially in English, then have a follow up project that takes care of the translations.

# WCMS Development Consulting

If there is a new WCMS being designed, or changes planned for an existing WCMS to support this project, the content strategist should be involved in the process. Don't worry, you won't be asked to design the content management system, but there is no reason that you can't inject yourself into that process as a subject matter expert. After all, you and your team are going to be the ultimate users of the WCMS so you have a legitimate right to ask to be a reviewer and approver of the WCMS work. Your success will largely depend upon how well designed the WCMS turns out to be.

Here are a few tips for advising on WCMS design:

* Ask about the necessity of all designed-in restrictions such as required fields and limitations on what can go into a content entry form. These things will almost always come back to bite you later. Let the authors and editors enforce consistency, not the WCMS.

* Get the WCMS design team thinking about the idea of system process time versus editorial work time. For a particular task in the WCMS, how much time is spent doing system-related tasks and waiting (process time) versus actually doing the editorial work (editorial work time). A good way to explain this is to ask how long it would take to create a new content item if the item was just one word. To create a content item with just one word, the author may have to

go through five or ten steps in the system and wait between each one. An example would be:

1. Create a new job in the system.
2. Go to the task list and start the job.
3. Enter any required metadata for the new content item.
4. Change to edit mode to create the content.
5. Type in the content.
6. Submit the content as complete.
7. Manually approve the content as part of the required workflow.
8. Wait for the new content item to show up in the folder for the project.
9. Publish the new content to create an HTML file.
10. View the new HTML file.

The only actual editorial work in that process was step 5, where the author types in the content. This task probably took two seconds. Performing all those other tasks in the system might take 5 minutes. Five minutes may not seem like a long time until you start to do the math on how many items you have that must go through that process. If you have 1000 content items to create and each one has 5 minutes of system time, not counting any writing or editing, then that's over two weeks of work time eaten up without any editorial work being performed at all. If there are external approvals or translations, this situation also causes these time estimate to go up.

Also, WCMS systems perform a lot of indexing and content associations behind the scenes and are very prone to slowing down when there are a lot of users. I worked on a project once with over twenty writers all creating new content in a brand new WCMS system and it became so slow that people were bringing in books and magazines to pass the time while they waited for the system to respond.

It is a good idea to add a business requirement specifying a maximum system time for a simple process with a normal number of users on the system. It is also a good idea to test this time every now and then as more users are added to the system.

Ask the WCMS designers if all the content entry forms they are creating are actually necessary. It is often better to have a few very flexible forms than many forms where each is designed to just create one kind of page or content module.

The Web Content Strategist's Bible

# Chapter 6 – Content Strategy During the Build Phase

The Build Phase is where the actual content development work is done. The project has been designed and that design has been approved and given the go ahead for development. During the Build Phase, the Content Strategist's main jobs are tracking the actual development of content, writing content, and editing/approving content. This phase is where many projects get off track without a Content Strategist or someone functioning as an editorial leader. If no one on the development team is tracking the progress of the content being written by the client, the team will be late every time. And again, without tracking, the team will not know that it is behind until it is too late to catch up to the project plan.

The actual content is the deliverable for this phase so there are no new documents to create other than what you might need for training.

# The Content Reviewer Guide

This document could be created as part of the Design Phase, but it is not uncommon to wait until the project goes into actual development. The Content Reviewer Guide is a training document to be given to everyone identified as a content reviewer for the project. It tells them exactly how to go about the approvals they must make. It is written as a step-by-step guide with screenshots where appropriate.

The steps to be described will differ by system used, but these items should be covered in some manner:

- How will reviewers be notified that there is content to review? Is there a system-generated email?
- How do reviewers log into the approval system?
- How do reviewers find out what their log in ID and password are if they forget?
- How do reviewers indicate that they would like to make a change? Can they change the content directly or just make comments?
- How do reviewers reject content that needs to be re-worked?
- What will happen if reviewers do not complete their approvals by the assigned date?
- What will happen if reviewers enter comments that conflict with another reviewer's comments?

# Content Strategist Tasks During the Build Phase

Since this phase is all about getting the actual work done, here are the things that a content strategist should be focusing on:

- **Prioritizing the work** – All content is not equal. It is the content strategist's task to figure out which kinds of content will take the longest to create, which are the most important and which must be created first because of dependencies. Once this is figured out, a prioritized list can be created so that the most critical content creation tasks are worked on first.

- **Assigning content development work** – If you are not doing all of the content development yourself, you will need to make clear content assignments to others. It is your job to make sure that everyone knows what to work on and when.

- **Tracking the work** – When the content development work begins, it will be the content strategist's job to keep track of how the work is progressing as compared to the project plan. To do this, all the content developers need to regularly report on their status.

- **Reporting the work status to management** – The content strategist should make regular reports on how the work is progressing to the project manager. This usually means reporting on percent of work that is complete and how that percentage matches against what was planned.

- **Prioritizing content issues** – The list of content-related things that can go wrong during development is endless. As each issue comes up, the content strategist should be involved in deciding if it is indeed and issue, and how critical it is to get it resolved. Not every problem has to be solved right now. Some things can wait for a maintenance release, and some issues can just be ignored.

## Maintaining the Content Matrix

**The importance of everyone keeping the content matrix up to date cannot be overstated.**

If there are several people doing content development, it might be a good idea to divide the matrix up and have each developer maintain that piece. If work is being done by someone outside of the content strategist's direct control, the strategist should probably keep control of the matrix and use it to track assignments and the completed content once delivered.

An up-to-date content matrix makes unexpected changes much easier to handle if, for example, someone quits or moves to another department in the middle of the project.

## Track and Complete the Project

Things will certainly go wrong during development. Content will be late, reviewers won't be available during the periods they committed to, and completely new sections of content may be needed. It happens all the time. But if you have a well-developed project plan, with agreed-upon contingencies, many arguments can be avoided.

The best you can do is to track everything carefully, so that when the unexpected happens, you know where you are in the plan. If content development is progressing ahead of schedule, then new content requests can be more easily accepted than if you are running late.

As changes do come up, always remember to go back to the basics of content planning. Figure out what new content is needed, how long each piece will take to complete, and who will do the work. Once you have this information, see how things fit within the expected timeline. If the development work just cannot be done, say so. It is often much easier to plan for a small follow up release right after the project launches than it is to risk the whole project by overworking the staff.

The Web Content Strategist's Bible

# Chapter 7 – Content Strategy During the Maintenance Phase

Once a new website is launched, it is out of date almost immediately. There may already be a waiting list of changes that need to be made that did not fit into the original project. A plan is needed for maintenance of the website content, the creation of new content for the site, and removal and archiving of old material on an ongoing basis.

Ignoring the Maintenance Phase is one of the mistakes I see most often in content strategy. This mistake results in lots of missed opportunities. First of all, the clients will love you for taking the initiative to do this work. It is usually something they won't even think about. But more importantly if you work for a Web development agency, by planning out all of the upcoming work that needs to be done on the website, you are identifying a lot of future work for your company. I once worked on a website for a large financial institution and at the end of the project I identified five large initiatives that the company was planning for the next year. My agency bid on, and won, all that work! Do you think that made my boss happy?

## Ongoing Website Maintenance

Here are three things that usually happen right after a new Web project launches:

- The project manager is left holding a list of minor defects that were not critical enough to be fixed before the project launched.
- External and internal users start viewing the new project and they find a list of new problems that were missed during testing.
- The project team that knows the content on the site better than anyone is either immediately put on another new project or, if they are contractors, let go.

As a content strategist, it is important to sit down with the project manager and the client/sponsor and resolve these issues before moving on to another project. The exact steps in the process will vary depending upon the size and scope of the project, but a good maintenance process should address these issues:

- **Staffing** – Now that the project team is gone, someone needs to be identified as responsible for handling the minor, ongoing maintenance changes. Ideally, this person should have been part of the development team, but if not, then a replacement should be identified early enough to train with the project team before the team is dispersed.

- **Tracking** – New defect reports will come in from everywhere. Customers will email, support staff will notice things that are wrong, and it seems like the CEO always finds a typo. A system needs to be put in place to capture all of these defects so they can be evaluated, ranked for importance, assigned, corrected, and tracked. If there are any outstanding known issues from before the project launched, these should also be entered into this system.

- **Schedule** – If someone on the technical team is responsible for actually putting new content up on the live production servers, then a schedule should be coordinated with this team so they know when to expect maintenance updates. Having a set schedule will make it possible for the maintenance team to give an approximate date when the problem will be corrected to the person that submitted the defect.

# Establishing an Editorial Calendar

Most large organizations have a lot of other things going on besides the current Web project. They probably have a list of planned changes for at least the next year.

New products may be in the works, expansions into new markets, etc. Many of these activities could have an impact on the Web project that was just completed.

The content strategist should talk with the client/sponsor and identify a good source within the organization for this kind of information (all within confidentiality agreements, and so on). The strategist should then create a calendar of planned for future changes to the website that includes:

- A brief summary of the coming campaign or announcement
- A description of the impact to the website
- The planned launch date
- An estimate of the number of hours of work needed for the website

This calendar should be turned over to whomever is tasked with the site's ongoing maintenance so the work can be planned and not come as a surprise.

If you are working for the client on contract, or as part of an agency, the client may, rightfully, be reluctant to release this kind of information to you. In this case, you should at least create the document structure and get the maintenance staff to complete the details.

## Content Removal Process Description

Getting new content loaded onto the live production server is a complicated process, but getting old content down off of the production server is a lot more complicated.

Before content is removed from the site, it is good practice to:

- **Make sure the page is not linked to from somewhere else in the website** - If you have a good site map that shows links, and you trust it, you could use it to identify any of your pages that link to the page being removed. If any are found, the referring pages will need to be updated to have the link changed or removed before the page can be deleted. If you do not have access to a complete linking structure document for the site, you can request that someone in the technical group run a GREP on the URL of the page to be deleted. GREP is short for *global-regular-expression-print*, a UNIX utility that allows the user to search one or more files for a specific string of text or filename and outputs all the lines that contain the string. This is another way to ensure that you won't be creating a broken link by removing a page.

- **Is there a redirect needed** – If there is concern that many users have bookmarked the page to be deleted, or it was referenced in old print material, then a redirect may be needed. A redirect is code that the technical team can put on the site to automatically send users requesting the deleted page to another page that is still available.

You should also document the process for submitting a request for content to be removed. It should specify:

- The process to be used to send a request to the technical team
- The format of the URL
- The testing and verification required
- The particular date on which you would like the content to be removed
- Other date-related restrictions, such as "do not remove before a certain date"

## Archival Plan and Policy

Most large organizations have some sort of document retention policy. Web documents should be subject to this policy. Consult the client/sponsor's legal department or compliance group to find out if a policy exists.

The National Archives issued guidelines for archiving Web content in 2005. This is a good place to start if you are unsure of archival requirements.

This document is located on the Web at:


**http://www.archives.gov/records-mgmt/policy/managing-web-records-index.html**

This guideline defines Web records that need to be maintained as:

Web content records:
- The content pages that compose the site, inclusive of the HTML markup
- Records generated when a user interacts with a site
- A list of the URLs referenced by the site's hyperlinks

Web management and operations records that provide context to the site include:
- Website design records
- Records that specify Web policies and procedures by addressing such matters as how records are selected for the site and when and how they may be removed
- Records documenting the use of copyrighted material on a site
- Records relating to the software applications used to operate the site
- Records that document user access and when pages are placed on the site, updated, and/or removed

Web management and operations records that provide structure related to the site include:
- Site maps that show the directory structure into which content pages are organized

- Software configuration files used to operate the site and establish its look and feel, including server environment configuration specifications

All archiving policies are not this inclusive, but this gives you some ideas to ask about.

# Chapter 8 – Content Strategy and Translations

Projects involving content that is to be translated have a much higher level of complexity and take a lot more time and resources to execute. It is much more complicated than just hiring an agency to perform the translations. The whole site development process has to be altered and the timelines extended or the plan must allow for a phased launch.

An entire book could be written just about handling translations alone, but surprising little has actually *been* written. Here are a few things that a content strategist needs to think about, keep in mind, define, and ask about when dealing with content that requires translation.

## Translation Impacts to the Project Plan

If the project has content that must go through a translation process, this must be accurately captured in the project plan. The translation portion of the plan should start after all of the content changes have been approved by the SMEs and the managing editor. It makes no sense to send content out for translation that is not final.

If a WCMS is being used to handle the workflow for content that has to be translated, make sure that you understand the entire process before you finalize the project plan. The most important question you need to ask the WCMS experts is; what happens to the source content while it is out for translation? In some cases, the source content is marked by the system as "Approved" before it is send out for translation. If this is the case, then content authors can continue to work on this content while it is being translated. They can publish the HTML, link to it, or run it back through workflow to add another country or language.

In other cases, the content is not marked as Approved until every language translation is complete. This will have an impact on the project plan if the source content pages are locked and cannot be published until after all translations are complete.

## Creating a Master Translation Glossary

Translating text from one language into another is as much an art as it is a science. There are usually many ways to say the same thing and express the same idea. The client/sponsor probably has dozens, if not hundreds, of words and phrases that it wants translated the same way every time. A good way to ensure this is to create a Master Translation Glossary that specifies the exact translation to be used for key words and phrases.

Some good candidates for the Master Translation Glossary are:

- The company name
- Marketing slogans
- Product names
- Product categories
- Common interface terms such as Help, Next, Back, etc.
- Application names
- Common field names such as, name, address, phone number, etc.

This document is usually created as a spreadsheet with the terms in the first row, language names as column headings, and the translated text for each term under its column heading. For example:

*Table 9 – Master Translation Glossary Example*

| English Term | Spanish | French |
|---|---|---|
| Help | Ayuda | Aide |
| Welcome | Bienvenido | Bienvenue |

This glossary can then be used by the translation vendor to ensure consistency, and also used by content authors if needed.

# Translation SME Issues

As mentioned earlier, it is not a good idea to just accept whatever is returned from a translation vendor without having someone in the organization verify the accuracy and appropriateness of the translated content. Most organizations task someone that is working in the region or country where the language is used to perform this check. This is the best way to handle this issue, but there are two problems that frequently arise:

- **The translation reviewer already has a full-time job besides reviewing translations.** If there is going to be a large amount of content translated, then it will also have to be reviewed. You must get an agreement from the translation reviewers and their bosses that they can be pulled away from their normal jobs for the time required in the project plan. This task could take a week or more, so it should be anticipated and planned for. This can be handled by good project planning.
- **The translation reviewers may want to perform a content review in addition to a translation review.** Most reviewers have a hard time with this one. They want to not only correct translation issues, but change the meaning of, add, or remove content as well. These kinds of changes need to be made to the source English content and any other language versions of the same content. If the change is just made only to, say the Spanish content, then the next time the English source

content is sent out for translation, this change will
not have been made in the source will not appear in
the translated Spanish version. This tendency to
make editorial changes can only be handled with
good training. If the translation reviewers see
problems with the factual accuracy of the content,
they should note this and report it to the content
team, not make changes themselves.

# Vendors and Translation Memory

Most large translation vendors use a Computer
Assisted Translation (CAT) system that retains previous
translation work they have performed for a client. When
they begin to do new translation work for this same client,
this CAT system is used to suggest a possible translation
for a phrase or sentence if it has been translated
previously. This repository of previously translated text is
referred to as Translation Memory and can be a big cost
saver for the client and a big time saver for the translation
vendor. The client is usually not charged for translations
used from translation memory as this cost has already paid
for in a previous translation.

An issue that is very often ignored until it is too late
concerns who owns the translation memory files? Most
clients assume that since it is their content, that it owns
this asset. These clients are frequently wrong. Unless it is
specifically stated in the contract, the vendor probably
owns this data. If you decide to leave and take your
translation work elsewhere, you cannot take the translation

memory file with you. The new vendor will have to start all over again and manually load your existing site into its system. Not owning your translation memory will have an affect on both cost and time. Be sure to get a definitive answer to this question before deciding to change translation vendors.

# Estimating Translation Word Counts

Estimating the number of words that will need to be translated is a black art. The bigger the project, the earlier you will have to make arrangements with a translation vendor so that it can have the appropriate language experts lined up and ready. The vendor will be asking for accurate estimates of word count changes for each language but most vendors cannot give you a good method for determining this estimate.

There are many factors that have to be taken into account. If you have used this vendor before, then it probably has a lot of content in translation memory, but exactly how much is anyone's guess. The best you may be able to do  for changes to content that has been previously translated, is to count all the words in each affected sentence, add up all the changes, then reduce the count by about 20 percent to account for translation memory savings. Sometimes translation memory automatically takes care of 75 percent of the changes and sometime almost none at all. There is just no way of knowing which it will be; so don't spend days worrying about the estimate.

# Specifying Languages and Countries

If you are working on a project that is being translated for the first time, there are a lot of questions that must be answered. The first is:

- **Do you want to specify the content by language or by country?** Specifying by language only may get you into trouble as the site grows. It is easy to say that the site needs to be in Spanish. But one size of Spanish does not fit all readers. Plus, you may need to have different content in Mexico than you have in Spain. Creating and storing your content based on the country will allow you to localize the content based on the country for which it is written, as well as localizing the language style. Argentinean Spanish spoken in South America is very different from Spanish spoken in Mexico and that is different from Castilian Spanish spoken in Spain.

- **What will your URL structure be?** If everything is written in English, then there is no need to worry too much about how the URL is built. But if you have multiple countries and languages it becomes much more important. Putting the country and language in the URL allows you to have content localized for each country at a URL that is varied by country. For example the URL for a page that lists all your products might look like this:

http://www.shooogle.biz/product_index.html

If you translate that page, how do you identify it by country or language? Changing the ending file name is one way. For example the URL could be .../product_index_mexico_spanish.html. If you are going to create the HTML manually and not use a WCMS, this might be a good system. In this case the source content (untranslated) file would be .../product_index_mexico_english.html. Once translated you would save it with the Spanish identifier.

If a WCMS is going to be used, then it is a better idea to include the country and language as different directories in the URL. For example, the URL would be:

http://www.shooogle.biz/mexico/spanish/product_index.html.

Specifying the country and language in the URL may allow you to use **dynamic content generation** functionality of the WCMS. This functionality allows you to have one source content file, product_index.html, and then change the content automatically based on the country. The process that allows this is called **metadata tagging**. Various WCSM systems handle this differently, but the idea is that you can associate all or part of the content on a page to a particular country. When the system generates the code for a page, it reads this metadata and only includes the content that you have listed as appropriate for a particular country. For example, here is a bulleted list of products:

Men's Shoes:
- Dress Shoes
- Athletic Shoes
- Casual Shoes
- Rain shoes

If Saudi Arabia is one of your targeted countries, you might choose to not tag the item "Rain Shoes" for inclusion in this market.

This is a very technical consideration, and not a decision that you would have to make by yourself. Just be aware that this is an issue that has to be discussed when translations are being considered.

# Internationalization vs. Localization

Ask a group of Web developers what they mean by the following terms and you will get very different answers:

- Internationalization
- Globalization
- Localization
- Translation

Which definition is right and which is wrong? There is a lot of confusion out there so for purposes of this discussion, here is what I mean when using the terms: **Internationalization/Globalization** – I use these terms interchangeably. This is the process of taking content that was written for a particular audience (English speakers in America) and re-writing it so that it can be easily understood by readers in any country. It often includes simplifying the grammatical syntax and removing idioms and figures of speech that are uniquely North American. For example the phrases "we will help your customers hit one out of the park" or "we will bend over backwards to make sure that you are successful" might seem very strange to even a native English speaker in India.

Internationalization/Globalization involves taking your source content and editing it so that it makes sense when literally translated into any language. When you are dealing with content that has been internationalized and then translated, then every language version is a direct, literal translation of the English source content.

---

The Web Content Strategist's Bible

**Localization** - The Localization Industry Standards Association (LISA) defines localization as follows:

> "Localization involves taking a product and making it factually and culturally appropriate to the target locale (country/region) where it will be used and sold." (http://www.lisa.org/)

There are two very different ideas in this definition—localization based on factual difference and localization based on cultural differences.

- **Factual Localization** forces you to have multiple version of the same exact content where the only differences are facts. For example let's say that you sell the exact same product in the U.S. and in China; however in the U.S. you offer a 90 day warranty and in China you offer a 30 day warranty. This may force you to have two versions of the product page that are identical except for the differences in warranty periods. These kinds of localization issues can be easily handled by a centralized content development team since these differences are easily understood and communicated.

- **Cultural Localization** is much harder to deal with. Once you start localizing your content based on subtle cultural differences, then the process of content development and maintenance becomes more complicated. With factual localization, an English speaking writer can easily create multiple versions of the content based on factual differences, get them translated to appropriate languages, and deploy the finished content. If a change needs to be made later, all that has to be done is to change each version in English and have the content re-translated. The writer does not need to have any special cultural knowledge.

Once you start localizing for differences that only a local writer would understand and be able to communicate, things get more difficult. Now, a centralized team of English speaking writers can no longer maintain your content. You either have to turn the content over to a local, culturally savvy, group of writers, or add a localization step into the process of maintaining the content. Adding this step greatly increases the cost and the time it takes to deploy content updates. When planning for localization, this needs to be taken into account.

For example, cultural localization for the Japanese market is a frequent problem for website developers in the United States. The direct and to-the-point writing style common in the U.S. is frequently viewed as impolite and offensive to a Japanese reader in a business context. If this is an issue, almost all of the content will have to be re-written by someone very familiar with Japanese customs and how business is conducted in Japan. This process will add extra time and cost to your project.

I worked on a site for a very large international U.S. corporation where this exact issue with Japan caused a huge stir. The corporation had a full-featured Japanese version of their website that was developed at no small cost. But when the marketing team from Asia visited the headquarters in the U.S., someone let it slip that they were so embarrassed by the Japanese version of the site that they refused to give the URL to customers. The marketing team in Japan went even further and paid a local firm to build a completely re-written, unauthorized version with which they felt more comfortable.

# Content Control

When translating a website's content for the first time, there are two models that can be used for ongoing site maintenance and updating. The two main models are **centralized control** or **distributed content control**. Each has its own advantages and disadvantages.

**Centralized control** emphasizes the single source idea. Content is written once (generally in English) in an internationalized style, then translated to as many countries and languages as are supported by the site.

The advantages of this model are:

- Consistency of message
- Centralized control
- Creation of content by non-language experts
- Response time for content updates
- Dedicated, centralized content staff

The disadvantages of this model are:

- Restriction of regional and country variation
- Rigidity of content
- Distance between content creators and content consumers

**Distributed Content** control turns the ongoing maintenance and updating of the content over to a writer/editor in the local regions.

The advantages of this model are:

- Messages that are finely tuned to local tastes and customs
- Proximity of content creators to the content consumers
- Frequent updates reflect local events, advertising, and holidays

The disadvantages of this model are:

- Insufficient workload to support a full-time, well-trained staff
- Lack of centralized control, once the content is translated and localized, executives in the central office will have no idea what the site says.
- Lack of synchronization with other regional versions of the site and the main corporate site
- Difficulty training a distant staff to used a complicated

Either model can be used very successfully depending upon the personality of the organization. Very structured organizations that prefer control will probably have issues with a distributed content model. A major corporation that I work with in the U.S. insists on total, centralized control of their website. They develop over one hundred localized versions of their site using a small, well-trained content staff and a powerful and complex WCMS. On the other hand, a major European auto manufacturer I consulted with was quite happy to turn large portions of their websites over to their local marketing staff and rarely even looked to see what they were saying online. In each case, the model worked well because it matched the personality and management style of the business.

## Translation Issues and the Content Strategist

If all of this is confusing to you, don't be alarmed. You won't have to make these decisions by yourself. The most important thing to get from this chapter is an idea of the process, the issues, and what kinds of questions to ask. As a content strategist, it is much more important to be able to ask the right questions at the right time than it is to have all the answers and try to dictate a solution.

# Chapter 9 – Search Engine Optimization and Content Strategy

A good content strategist should know the basics of writing for SEO (search engine optimization. Basically, SEO is the process of changing and adjusting a Web pages content and technical structure with the goal of improving how the page is ranked by search engines such as Google, Yahoo, and MSN. Dozens of books have been written on the subject and huge consulting businesses have been built around SEO, so I can only scratch the surface here. But frankly, what a good Web writer and content strategist needs to know is not that complex.

SEO is usually a secondary project that is run once the initial Web site has been launched and has had some time to be included in the indexes of the various search engines. But performing some of this work during the initial content development for the site is a very smart idea.

## Focus on Google

There are a lot of search engines, and they all use different criteria to decide how to rank and present all of the pages in their index that correspond to an individual search request. At this time Google gets about 70% of all search traffic (http://www.hitwise.com/press-center/hitwiseHS2004/leader-record-growth.php). So until that changes, it just makes good sense to focus on improving your search results in Google with the assumption that if you improve in Google that you will also likely improve in the other search engines.

## What Pages Should Be Optimized?

When a client, or someone on your team, comes to you for advice on SEO, the first question to ask is – What pages need to be optimized? Every page on the site does not have to optimized for SEO, and many will just naturally optimize themselves. If there is a Privacy Policy page on Shoogle.com, and someone searches for the phrase "Shoogle privacy policy" in Google, that page will probably just naturally appear as the first search result because it is so specific to Shoogle that there are not many other pages on the entire Internet that contain that phrase. But product pages generally take more work. If Shoogle.com wants to get a Web page to appear on the first page of search results for the phrase "work boots", they will have to do a lot of work. Right now, there about 500,000 pages indexed by Google that contain the phrase "work boots." That's a lot of competition for the top spots.

## SEO Revolves Around Keywords

Keywords are the words or phrases that users type into Google, or another search engine, when looking for information. In the above example, the keyword phrase was, "work boots." So all of the SEO effort will involve trying to improve search results for a particular set of keywords.

In the context of SEO, "high ranking" is anything on the first page of search results (the first ten items returned). Anything lower than the third page (30 results) will get so little traffic that it is considered to be "non-ranking."

**High Ranking** = A search result in the top 10 results

**Ranking** = A search result somewhere in the top 30 search results

**Non-ranking** = No result, or any search result beyond the first 30

Whether you are being asked to optimize a few existing pages, and existing Web site, or a completely new Web site, the process is pretty much the same.

# Keyword Focused SEO Process

For a keyword-focused approach, you start with a list of keywords, see how the site is doing for those keywords, then adjust. The process goes like this:

1. Create a list of keywords that are important to the business.

2. Test all of the keywords to see what the search results are for each keyword.

3. Identify keywords for which your site is not returning any results or has low ranked results.

4.  Match these keywords that need improvement to individual pages or your site, or create new pages for them.

5.  Use SEO techniques to adjust these pages.

6.  Retest and see if the changes made an improvement in the search results.

7.  Repeat.

## Step 1 – Creating the Initial Keyword List

Your first step is to create a spreadsheet listing all the keywords you can think of that might be important to the project at hand. The goal is to get at least 50 keywords for a small project and about 300 for a large project. Here are a few ideas for finding keywords and phrases to add to your list:

- **Branded product names**. If your company or client creates or manufactures specific product with branded, copyrighted names, you definitely want to make sure that you get very high-ranking search results.

- **Other branded terms** – Words and phrases such as the company name, nick names such as "Big Blue" for IBM, and slogans, such as "The tightest ship in the shipping business" should also be added to the list.

- **Product categories** – If the client's products break down into broad, well-defined categories, such as "work boots," then add those to the list.

- **Search logs** – If there is an existing Web site and it has a search feature, then the terms that users are entering to search for are all collected in a search log file that your technical team should be able to give you to analyze. It is critical to find out how your customers are looking for your products. Everyone in your company may call them "work boots," but if the majority of your customers call them "construction boots," then you are not going t be optimizing for the correct keywords.

- **Brainstorm** – Think of as many other keywords and phrases as you can and add them to the list.

- **Google External Keyword Tool** – There are many tools online that can help you explore and identify more keywords. One of the most used in the Google External Keyword Tool (https://adwords.google.com/select/KeywordToolExternal). Enter a word or phrase that describes the project, and the tool will return a list of hundreds of similar words and phrases that you might not have thought of.

Add all of these keywords to a spreadsheet, then sort the keywords alphabetically and scan and remove duplicates. If you have come up with more than 300 to 400 keywords, you probably want to trim a few words out and keep them for a second project so that you can have a reasonable number of keywords to work with.

## *Step 2 – Test the Initial Keyword List*

Now that you have your initial list of keywords for which you want the project to rank, you need to set a baseline. Before you start changing things on the site to try to improve search results you need to know how the Web page is currently doing. You will need this later to compare and see if things are getting better or worse.

For each keyword or phrase in your list, go to Google, enter the words and record the results in your keyword spreadsheet. You want to record the **position number**, the **page title**, and the **URL** returned for any pages on your Web site in the first 100 results. If you enter a keyword and there are no pages from your site in the top 100 results, list the keyword ranking as 101. You will be able to use these values to sort the list by ranking position. Ignore the Sponsored Links at the top of the search results page.

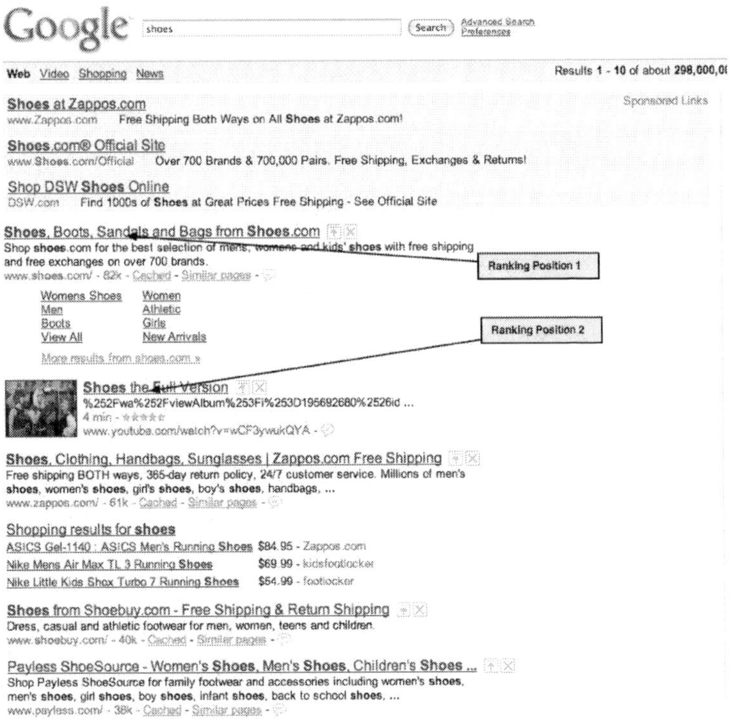

*Figure 3 How to identify ranking position in Google Results. Ignore the paid results at the top.*

## Step 3 – Identify Keywords That Need Improvement

Now that you know which pages in your site are being returned when you search for each keyword, you can refine your keyword list. To do this, go into your keyword spreadsheet and sort the list by the Ranking Position column so that the list is in order by ranking position from 1 down to 101.

The Web Content Strategist's Bible

For the first round of SEO work, you should focus on all the keywords that are not in the first ten positions in search results, all keywords with a ranking in 11 or greater.

You can always come back later and work on the keywords that are already in the top ten spots to try and move them into the number one slot.

## Step 4 - Match the Keywords that Need Improvement to Individual Web Pages

Now we need to make sure that the page that we are tracking in the search results is the *right page* for that keyword. Very often the page that is the highest-ranking page on your site for a keyword is not the page that you would want customers to see first. For example, with the keyword "work boots," if the first page on your site that shows up in search results is an old press release and not the product category page for Work Boots, then the wrong page is being ranked highest.

For each keyword where this is the case, go back into Google and see where, or if, the correct page shows up in search results at all. Replace the existing URL in your spreadsheet for this keyword and change the ranking position.

For every keyword that is listed as "non-ranked," identify the page in your site that you would like to be ranked highest for this keyword and enter that URL in your spreadsheet.

At the end of this step, you should have a URL listed for every keyword that identifies the page on your Web site that you would like to be returned in the number one position when customers search for that keyword in Google. These are the pages that you will be changing to try and improve search results ranking.

## *Step 5 - Use SEO Techniques to Adjust these Pages*

For each page identified as needing optimization, use these SEO techniques. **Things that can be done to improve search engine results fall into two categories**:

- **On-page Factors** – Content contained in the page itself and the HTML code for that page
- **Of-page Factors** – Things that are not part of the HTML and content for a Web page such as technical issues and site structure and how the page is linked to both inside your site and from external sites

For this simple SEO project we will focus on on-page factors since we have complete control over them.

## On-Page SEO Factors

On-page SEO factors fall into two groups – **metadata** and **page content.**

## Metadata Factors to Adjust

As we discussed earlier, metadata is loosely defined as data about data. In this case, you will need to learn just a little bit about HTML. Web pages built using HTML have two main parts, the HEAD and the BODY. Search engines look at both parts to determine what the page is about and for which keywords it should rank highly. The HEAD area contains a few lines called Meta tags. If you are creating HTML using a Web Content Management System (WCMS) then you probably have access to the meta tag content and can make changes to try to improve search results. If your technical team builds the HTML pages, you can just submit your changes to them for inclusion in the page code.

So lets look at each important meta tag and see how we can use content in these tags to improve search results.

### &lt;title&gt;

**The title tag in the HEAD is the most important tag in regards to search results**. Note that this is not content that is viewed in the body of the Web page, but it will be visible as the text used at the very top of your browser window.

### &lt;title&gt; Tag Tips

**Example - &lt;title&gt;**Work Boots & Construction Boots – Shoogle.com, at least 20% savings on shoes every day**&lt;/title&gt;**

- Use the most relevant and important keywords in the title, even before the company name.

- Each Web page should have it's own, unique title content containing the keywords for which you want that page to rank highly.

- The title tag content should not exceed 120 characters, nothing beyond that will be used by the search engines.

- In Google, only the first 66 characters will be visible to the user in the browser title area (all 120 will be used to determine ranking), but Yahoo displays all 120 characters.

## &lt;description&gt;

The description meta tag is mostly ignored in the calculation of search engine ranking, but the search engines may present the content of your meta description tag as the text used on the search result page. So entice the user to click on the search result by using interesting and relevant copy here.

### &lt;description&gt; Tag Tips

Example - &lt;META NAME="description" CONTENT="The very best Work & Construction Boots from Shoogle.com. Receive at least a 20% savings on top brands such as XXXXX and YYYY every day."&gt;

- Include your primary keywords at the beginning of the text.

- Limit the description to 200 characters.

- Avoid repeating the same word over and over again

- Create a unique description for each Web page.

### &lt;keywords&gt;

This keywords meta tag lists the words or phrases about the contents of the Web page. This tag provides some additional text for crawler-based search engines. However because of frequent attempts to abuse their system, most search engines ignore this tag.

Carefully choose the keywords you insert into meta tags. List keywords you think people might typically use.

### &lt;keywords&gt; Tag Tips

**Example - &lt;META NAME="keywords"**
**CONTENT="**boots,work boots,construction boots,steel toe,safety,shoes,footware,Timberland,Pit Boss"&gt;

- Include popular synonyms of your keywords (since search engines are now extracting keywords from text, the inclusion of synonyms is one of the most important uses of keyword meta tags).

- Include common misspellings of the keywords.

- Limit the number to around 20 keywords or phrases.

- Separate each entry with a comma; a space is not needed after the comma.

- Avoid repeating the same word or phrase over and over again (a few times is OK).

## Geo Location Meta Tags

As location-based searching becomes more popular, adding these meta tags has become more important. If your physical location is important to your customers ( your office, store, restaurant, etc.), adding these tags is a must. Anyone who has an iPhone knows the benefit of having a device that knows where you are and can find things that are close to you. Location-based searching is going to be very important. Google Local Search is also booming so if you have a Web site for a Pizza restaurant in Roswell GA, you certainly want to come back high in search results when someone enters the phrase "pizza roswell, ga" into Google.

The exact method for identifying your location to the various search engines has yet to be agreed upon. To be safe, it is best to include several different kinds of meta tags. Below is a list of good tags to start with.

**Example Tags:**

```
<meta name="zipcode" content="30076">
<meta name="city" content="Roswell">
<meta name="state" content="Georgia">
<meta name="geo.region" content="US-
GA">
<meta name="geo.placename"
content="Roswell, GA">
<meta name="geo.position"
content="34.038529, -84.343111">
<meta name="ICBM" content="34.038529, -
84.343111">
```

The geo.position and ICBM tags require your latitude and longitude. The easiest way to get the latitude and longitude numbers is from Google Maps.

1. Go to maps.google.com
2. Enter your complete address and click on "Search Maps"
3. When your location pops up, don't zoom or move the map, just type the following code string into your browser:

```
javascript:void(prompt('',gApplication.getMa
p().getCenter()));
```

4. You'll get a popup with the coordinates!

Use your main keywords for your site in your URL if possible. Sometimes this causes branding issues, but it helps with SEO. For example, www.shoogle_shoes.com would help with SEO for the keyword "shoes" but may not be that great for branding. This can be overcome by using keyword terms in your site's directory structure such as: www.shoogle.com/shoes/index.html.

## Page Content Factors to Adjust

Page Content factors are things you can change in the textual content that is displayed to the user on your Web page. This is the actual text on the page.

### Headings

The search engines pay particular attention to text that is defined as a heading. Headings are defined in the HTML code by surrounding the text with a <H1> through <H5> tag. The <H1> tag is the highest level, displays the largest font, and usually the page title. Using heading tags, rather than manually making some text bold or a larger font, helps the search engines understand the structure of your page and what words are most important to the user.

## <H1> through <H5> Tag Tips

**Example - <H1>Construction and Work Boots</H1>**

- Headings also make good links.

- Don't use graphics or graphical text as headings since the search engines cannot read the content

- Use headings often to divide the page into logical chunks. Headings help both the search engines and your readers.

### Keyword Placement in the Content on the Page

You must use the main keyword for which you want to rank in the body of the content on the page. The search engines will scan the headings and the page content when trying to determine what the page is about and how to index and rank it.

## Keyword Placement and Page Content Tips

- Use your main keywords in the first sentence of the first paragraph.

- Use your main keywords two or three more times throughout the body of the page

- Use the main keyword phrase again in the last sentence.

- Call out your main keyword phrase once with bold text and once with italics text.

- More content on the page is better than less. Each important page should have at least 200 to 400 words. All other things equal, the page with the most content will probably rank higher.

### Links

Search engines also pay particular attention to the text used to link to pages on your Web site. This includes internal links from one page to another.

Whenever possible, use your main keywords in links pointing a page on your site.

**Use this structure**:

More information on <u>Work and Construction Boots</u>

**Rather than this structure**:

Click <u>Here</u> for more information on Work and Construction Boots

---

Having the link text (Work and Construction Boots) closely match the main keywords on a page reinforces the importance of those keywords.

## Step 6 - Retest and See if the Changes Improved in the Search Results

After you have made all the SEO changes to all the pages, give the search engines a week or so to crawl the site again and re-rank your pages. Then, for each keyword in your spreadsheet, go back and list the new ranking position, note any improvement, and list what you did to cause the improvement.

Resort the list by the new rankings column.

## Step 7 - Repeat

If needed, you can now go back and repeat this process for any keywords on your list. Try making a few more tweeks to the pages and test the results.

The Web Content Strategist's Bible

# Chapter 10 – What You Need to Know about Web Content Management Systems

## Why Is It Important to Know about Web Content Management Systems?

Every project does not need a content strategist. Some projects have very little editorial content, or are re-using existing content, or are just very small. However, large, complex projects need a content strategist. These projects have lots of content and lots of moving parts for which someone has to estimate time and cost and monitor stages of completion. These are also the projects that are most likely to have a Web content management system (WCMS) as part of the customer solution. Show me a project that needs a WCMS, and I'll show you a project that needs a content strategist.

## What Is a Web Content Management System?

Web Content management systems (WCMS) are software and database packages that allow an organization to easily create and update website and Intranet content. This can mean many things depending on the organization's mission and size. Generally speaking, content management primarily reduces repetitive manual work such as HTML coding, and even copying/pasting text across documents. Additional efficiencies are gained by reducing repetitive management tasks such as sending version approvals, maintaining schedules, creating task lists and other activities. The text is stored in a database and eventually used to generate finished HTML Web pages without the need for a programmer. This kind of control allows the communications department to take back control of the website from the IT organization.

The biggest issue facing WCMS users today is the lack of a universal standard. There is no Microsoft Word® for content management systems. Some of you may remember back when your résumé might get tossed because you didn't have WordPerfect or Bookmaster experience. It mattered because they worked very differently from each other and from Microsoft Word. The interfaces were different. One was a WYSIWYG system and the other forced you to use markup tags similar to HTML. Just because you could use one didn't mean that you could use the other. In some ways, the WCMS market today is even worse. There are more players and almost every installation is customized. So even if you have worked on a website that uses a popular system, you might not even recognize the same system when customized for use by another organization for another website.

For the purpose of understanding content strategy and getting a job as a content strategist, it's *more important* that you understand the idea behind a Web content management system than have minor experience using one.

To be able to understand the editorial work for a project, and convince a potential boss that you should be considered for a position, you really only need to understand four ideas about Web content management:

- Separating Content from Presentation
- Managing and creating metadata
- Using and designing content input templates
- Using work flow automation

# Separating Content from Presentation

Textual Web content and its presentation are inextricably linked in viewers eyes. Yet content is often reused in website, Intranet or other documents in many different contexts. For example, legal disclaimers appear at the bottom of HTML press releases or PDF product sheets. Product specifications may find themselves into Flash presentations and XML documents.

As an organization's content and knowledge grow, writing content separately from presentation (i.e., layout, style, document format, etc.) is essential to promoting cost-effective communications.

Consider this extreme example: a hypothetical website that has 5,000 individual documents (HTML files) and uses any one of 10 different page layouts. Now imagine that the website graphic design must change within the day. Sound impossible? It would be if the formatting was all mixed in with the text. But if the two are separate then it's just a matter of changing the code that controls the presentation and the rest is pretty easy. As corporations constantly re-brand and merge, this kind of flexibility is essential.

# Metadata

The simple definition of **metadata** is that it is data about other data. That definition rarely satisfies anyone, so let's take a more concrete example—an automobile. Metadata about a car would be:

- Who owns it now?
- Who owned it before?
- How many miles has it been driven?
- What is its maintenance record?

A tire would not be metadata, because it is part of the car.

For a content record stored in a WCMS, metadata might be:

- How is this content record identified?
- Who created the file?
- When was it last edited?

- If it is used on multiple pages, what are they?
- For which countries is this content written and into what languages will it be translated?
- Is the content approved or pending approval?

All of this is important information that the system can use to help manage the content. For example, if the content is pending approval, the system may prevent anyone else from making edits or changes. Every WCMS relies on metadata to manage the state and movement of the content it contains. There is no way you can know what particular metadata might be used for any project, but understanding the concept is important.

# Input Templates

Actual content text gets entered into a WCSM using input templates. Like metadata, these templates will be customized and will be unique to every site depending upon the content contained on a particular page and the purpose of the website. These templates are simply structured forms with blank spaces into which a content author types or pastes text.

A simple input template for a page that has a title, a heading, some body text and a link might be as simple as this:

Page Title: _____

Heading: _____

Body Copy:

Link Text: _____

Link URL: _____

Page URL: _____

*Figure 4 – WCMS Input Template Example*

An input template for a complex product page in an online catalog might have fifty input fields and allow for many paragraphs of text.

The important thing about capturing textual data in this manner is that it allows for easy re-use of previously created content. The example above might have one more field labeled "**CMS Module**" to be used by the author to enter a WCMS identifier (file name) for an existing module of text and it would appear on the Web page. "Write the content once, and use it in a lot of places" is the current WCMS philosophy. If the content changes, you only have to make the edit in one place and the change appears everywhere that the module is used.

## Work Flow Automation

Most large WCMS programs operate on a job-based work flow method. To work in the system, you need to start by creating a job. The job contains a lot of information about what it is you are going to do in the system. By creating a job, you are not just saying "I want to edit content record X"; you are saying, "I want to edit this content; I want John, and Tim, and Sue to look at it and approve it; I want to send it out for translation into these five languages; I want someone to verify the translation; and I want to publish the finished content to this specific directory on this date." Specifying all these details in the job lets the system automatically take care of routing files around and keep track of where everything is. Again, work flow systems differ from one WCMS to another, and from one implementation of a single WCSM to another, but understanding the idea will help get you a job as a content strategist.

## Who Are the Big Players?

While there is still no one system that dominates the market, there are a few big players that you should know about. Again, just knowing these names will put you way ahead of most in the pack. If you want to make sure that you are up on all the latest industry buzzwords, check out the following product descriptions.

## *Interwoven TeamSite*

(http://www.interwoven.com/components/page.jsp?topic
=PRODUCT::TEAMSITE)

From Interwoven's website, here is the product
description:

### Web content management: Interwoven TeamSite

- Ensure brand consistency across all Web
  and application touch points and improve
  customer satisfaction and loyalty
- Consolidate dozens of Web properties into a
  single managed environment to drive down
  expenses and accelerate time to market
- Empower business users to manage their
  own content for faster changes with less
  overhead
- Reuse content across business applications
  and sites to improve consistency and reduce
  publishing costs
- Enforce compliance with Web and corporate
  standards through automated review and
  approvals and by archiving auditable copies
  of all Website versions

Interwoven TeamSite Content Management
delivers the foundation that businesses need to
build, deploy, and integrate content across the
enterprise.

Interwoven TeamSite is the industry's most advanced content management platform for the enterprise. TeamSite underpins a wide range of enterprise applications—from intranets and internal portals to public Websites, dealer portals and extranets—that businesses rely on. That is why the world's most successful companies, including GE, Siemens, and Cisco Systems, have standardized on TeamSite as the foundation for managing their high-value information assets.

Based on patented, award-winning, sixth-generation technology, Interwoven TeamSite enables organizations to manage virtually any content type for any purpose, including multi-channel publishing, for consistent content across the Web, wireless, e-mail, and print. TeamSite seamlessly integrates with leading portal platforms and enterprise applications including IBM®, BEA®, SAP®, Plumtree® Siebel®, and PeopleSoft®.

## *Vignette*

(http://www.vignette.com)

Here is the product description:

Web content management technology evolved with the Web to meet the needs of large-scale, complex Web sites. Vignette was and remains one of the world's leading providers of this technology. We became leaders by envisioning Web content management as a strategic business tool focused on improving operational agility, individual empowerment and organizational growth. All enterprises know that customers, partners, suppliers and employees require efficient access to the most current information. Vignette understands that to deliver the most superior online experience possible, Web content management solutions must support the effective creation and management of Web content, automate Web-related processes, deliver the right content in the right context, and continually analyze Web presence efficacy. Our customers have achieved operational excellence and reduced costs by consolidating Web sites that expose silos of information with ease and security.

Today, enterprises are re-examining their use of the Web and Web technologies, seeking opportunities for renewed innovation. As these organizations attempt to define their next-generation Web presence, they are also rethinking their technology requirements. Vignette, the industry's leading Web content management provider, continues to maintain its leadership position in this next-generation Web.

Vignette's Web content management solutions:

- Empower business users to directly manage Web content and the on-line experience without burdening IT
- Uniquely provide native management and delivery of all electronic assets
- Offer unique dynamic delivery of the right content to the right person in the right context
- Reduce risk and deliver a consistent Web experience through intelligent publishing
- Adhere to evolving industry standards like XML, J2EE, .NET and Web services

## *Documentum*

(http://software.emc.com/products/product_family/docu
mentum_family.htm)

The ECM Documentum family of products is so complex
that the website does not even attempt to describe
everything in one place. Here is a very high-level
description of the Documentum product family:

> The EMC Documentum product family helps you
> manage all types of content across multiple
> departments within a single repository. With a
> unified repository, various groups can easily share
> and reuse their content with other areas of the
> business that would benefit from access to this
> valuable information. Our product family also
> allows your business to share its content safely with
> outside organizations including partners, vendors,
> and customers.

This description then goes on to describe seventy
individual products and services that can be used to satisfy
very specific requirements such as publishing content for
Blackberry clients etc.

---

# Why Is Understanding WCMS So Important?

There are many writers out in the market looking for work. There are many with more experience than you. There are many who are willing to work for a much lower rate than you. But there are very, very few writers who know anything at all about Web content management systems, and the ones who have this knowledge earn a higher rate of pay and are rarely without work.

The Web Content Strategist's Bible

# Chapter 11 – Getting Your First Job as a Web Content Strategist

If you are convinced that Web content strategy is something you would like to try, the goal is probably closer than you think. If you have any kind of writing background, you are more than half the way there. You probably understand a lot about the writing process and have some useful experience.

The most important advice I can give you regarding your job search is:

**Don't believe everything you read in Web Content Strategist's job descriptions.**

---

Three-quarters of the "requirements" listed are probably "nice to have" but not essential, or are just standard boiler plate. Every company wants a "self-starter" who can "work well without supervision." Don't worry too much about the long list of qualifications cited. Go ahead and apply. A well-written and designed résumé and cover letter may be all it takes to get your foot in the door.

Follow these steps to get ready to start looking for a job as a Web content strategist:

1.  Look at how you describe your previous work in your résumé . Your previous job titles are very important. The first thing a resume reviewer looks at is your previous experience. You need to emphasize any Web experience, preferably in the position title. For instance, if you did writing and editing for anything that wound up on the Web, break that out and list your title as Web Writer. If you edited the work of others, list this on a separate line as Web Editor. Don't make things up, but be sure to play up any work you have done for a Web audience.

2.  Most résumés are stored digitally these days so they can be searched. To help potential clients find you, make sure you use these magic words:

    Web content
    Content Strategist
    Web
    Internet
    Content Matrix
    Content Management

The Web Content Strategist's Bible

WCMS

If you have done anything like tracking writing work with a spreadsheet, call it out and refer to the document as a "matrix." This has a special meaning in the Web design and development world. These are the words for which clients are searching when looking for Web content strategy help. Use as many of them as you can even if they only appear in the description of the kind of job you are seeking.

3.   Craft a strong cover letter, again using as many of the magic words listed above as possible and calling out any applicable experience. I'm always amazed at how many applicants fail to take a few minutes to write a simple, targeted cover letter.

4.   Develop a few good samples of your work. It's very important to have a sample of a content matrix in your portfolio. So if you have never built one before, create something to use as a sample. If you are applying for a job with a specific company, look at its existing website and create a basic matrix for a small part of the site. A trick that has worked for me is to look at the source code for each Web page (in Internet Explorer, select the **View** menu then select **Source**) and look in the first few lines of code for something that might be the unique identifier for that page and list it in your matrix. This is just one more thing that will set you apart from other candidates. Don't worry too much about making up a content matrix, you are just showing the potential client that you understand the idea.

5. Create a simple branding scheme to tie all of your documents together visually. This is a huge step that most people miss. Think about your audience; these are creative design and communications people. They care about how things look and design consistency. You want to be able to sit down across a desk from an interviewer and hand them a folder containing a cover letter, a résumé, a list of references (if you have them), and samples that have the same design and appearance. You don't have to go overboard here, but just find one or two little design elements and use them consistently across all your documents. I was quite successful doing something as simple as making the first letter of my name red and using brackets creatively here and there. You don't have to do much because almost no one else will go to the trouble.

6. Build PDF files out of all of these documents so they can be quickly and easily emailed or uploaded.

7. Save an unformatted, text only version of your résumé to be used on the major job websites like Monster.com and CareerBuilder.com. This version should have no formatting besides carriage returns to make sure things line up correctly. Don't rush through this version. The text-only, online version of your resume is usually a recruiter's first exposure to you and your attention to detail. If you are sloppy with this document, they will assume that all your work is equally sloppy and pass you by.

An added bonus would be to have all of your documentation and samples available online in a website, but only go this far if you are already comfortable building and designing websites. It's not necessary, will take too much time if you are learning, and could do more harm than good if a poorly designed and built.

# Finding Web Content Strategist Jobs

You should target three groups when looking for Web content strategist jobs:

- Large corporations
- Web design studios
- Technical and marketing contracting companies

When just starting out, a good place to concentrate is the third category—companies that provide short-term workers on contract. These companies already have the connections to companies in your area and have access to many jobs that are never posted on any job board. Find these companies by looking online and by looking at job ads posted on the big job websites like Monster and CareerBuilder. Many of the listings will be placed by contracting companies who will be happy to have your résumé in the database. Contact these companies directly and let them know that you are seeking contract work as a Web writer/editor or Web content strategist. They probably won't know what that means, but if your résumé has the right keywords, it will come up when they are searching for résumés to send to their clients.

If you get contacted by a contracting company to go on an interview with a client, be sure to bring along your package of nicely designed and formatted documents and samples. What the potential client gets from the contracting company will be pretty basic and unattractive. Be sure to leave a nice copy of your work with the client following your interview.

Once you have contacted contracting companies in your area, start working on any Web design studios in your area or nearby cities. Again, the easiest way to work for these companies is to start on contract. Look them up on the Web and see if you can find a name and address. Send them a nice cover letter introducing yourself as a local Web writer/editor and content strategist. Web design studios often hire these people on contract for a specific project as they usually don't have enough work to keep a staff of Web writers and strategists around as full-time employees.

You may have to take a job or two as a Web writer to build up your portfolio and experience, but eventually a content strategist job will come along. Once you get your foot in the door with a couple of clients, you will probably have all the work you can handle.

## The Right Attitude

Here is a final word or two about attitude. Once you get an interview and are sitting across the table from an interviewer, a good, positive attitude will get you further than you might think. If someone has taken the time to call you in to meet, the company is probably already satisfied with your qualifications. Now the hiring manager just wants to meet you and see how you might fit with the project team.

Here are a few things that impress me when I am interviewing Web content strategist candidates:

- **You really want this particular job and want to do this particular kind of work.** Few things will turn me off faster than someone who just wants any job in the Web field. I want to hire someone who really wants to work in the Web content area. It takes a long time and a lot of effort to train someone new; so a manager wants to find someone who would be willing to stick around if the opportunity presents itself and there is a good fit with the team. The manager is probably not going to tell you this during the interview, but the thought is there.

- **You are confident in your ability to learn.** Learning a new website and new Web content management system is always a challenge. Experience has shown most hiring managers that a large percentage of writers do not have the technical aptitude to  pick it up and be successful. Without being cocky, show the manager that you are confident that you will be able to learn whatever is needed.

- **You don't apologize or belittle your background.** If you have weak areas or missing qualifications, don't bring them up unless the hiring manager asks about them. If asked, just highlight your positive experience, explain your understanding of the area in question, and be confident that it won't be a problem.

# The Jobs Are There

I see new job openings all the time and more projects are using a content strategist as part of the core team. As with any career field, persistence and networking pay off. If there is an interactive marketing organization in your area, join and go to the events. Meet people, get your name out there, and the work will come. It's a fun creative, and exciting career field with a lot of potential growth. If you want it, it's certainly there for the taking.

# Appendix A – Supporting Research

The information presented in this book regarding best practices for Web writing is backed by industry research. I often reference these studies when offering a critique of a client's current website content. The two seminal studies by Morkes and Nielsen in the late 1990s were so well done and highly regarded that more recent research is hard to come by.

## Morkes and Nielsen, 1997

The first study completed by John Morkes and Jacob Nielsen in 1997

---

(http:www.useit.com/papers/webwriting/writing.html) found that:

- When a sample website was rewritten for scannabilty, user scores improved **47 percent**
- When a sample website was rewritten for conciseness, user scores improved **58 percent**
- When a sample website was rewritten for objectivity, user scores improved **28 percent**
- And when all three methods were used, user scores improved **124 percent**.

The scores were based on:

- Task time
- Task errors
- Content recall
- Subjective experience

Test subjects were both technical and non-technical users.

## Morkes and Nielsen, 1998

A second study completed in 1998 by Morkes and
Nielsen
(www.useit.com/papers/webwriting/rewriting.html)
showed even more improvement when the Web pages were
also edited for better internal navigation and split into
logical sub-pages. The results of this study showed
improved scores of **159 percent** when combined with the
editorial elements of scannability, conciseness, and
objectivity.

## Princeton Survey Research

## Associates, 2000

(http://www01.screamingmedia.com/en/content_servic
es/why_content/data.php)
Once they become Internet users, Americans rely heavily
on the Internet as a source of information, and come to
view it as more indispensable to their lives than television
or newspapers.  They also trust the information they get

online as much, or more, than the information they get from other sources, and typically view the Internet as offering more up-to-date, in-depth, interesting information than the other media types.

This survey suggests that the Internet has reached a new level of maturity as a source of information for users and should no longer be perceived as a secondary, or second-class, medium. Internet users are surprisingly zealous converts.

The Web Content Strategist's Bible

# Appendix B – Content Strategist Job Duties and Descriptions

The kinds of duties that could be assigned to a content strategist are many and varied. Here, in no particular order, are the kinds of duties and responsibilities I've seen in recent content strategist job ads I've written and read.

- Conduct content strategy and writing activities, including internalizing user needs and business objectives, creating content / message briefs, writing content outlines and flow charts, writing copy decks, conducting content audits

- Work with design and information architecture (IA) leads, project managers and producers to integrate content with larger user experience
- Participate with other project team members on project definition activities, including business requirement gathering, current application assessment, competitive analysis, usability assessment, ethnographic and other types of field research, and secondary research
- Deliver quality presentations and answer client questions
- Gather business and technical requirements
- Analyze user and business needs
- Define user requirements
- Develop content inventories and assessments
- Develop editorial platforms (style guides)
- Write, edit, and proof content
- Develop and modify standards and guidelines

The Web Content Strategist's Bible

- Facilitate user-centered participatory design sessions

- Set strategy for how content should be added, deleted, upgraded on a continual basis—which product lines, which industries, how much should we have, how should it be organized on the sites, do we need matching sets of items or just a single product, etc.

- Prioritize projects using data analysis and forecasting techniques based on economic value to the company

- Set metrics for measuring the success of new content after launch. Track and report new content sales results

- Work with Product Managers to understand product strategies, target customers, and launch dates for new products (i.e. when new content needed). Suggest new products that can be merchandised purely by developing new content for existing products

- Track trends in key industries and among competitors. Conduct market research on Content to use as input into overall strategy and creative briefs

- Work with the global marketing team to set strategy for country-specific content

- Hire, train, and manage a team of content managers and associates

- Consult with internal stakeholders (product marketing managers and communications managers) to understand and assess their strategic business needs relative to the corporate web sites, including intranet and external customer-facing properties. This includes convening and leading a cross-functional web planning or project initiation team with the business unit.

- Develop and implement an annual web initiatives plan and budget for content and functional development as well as web research that aligns with corporate, business and marketing/communications plans and strategies.

- Work directly with corporate web team to manage projects collaboratively and integrate content and design with corporate brand standards, web architecture and technology. Meet regularly to keep projects on track and communication lines open

- Manage outside vendor relationships as they relate to web development and maintenance of web content or functionality

- Develop a content creation plan

- Provide guidance to client copywriters when necessary

- Evaluate existing content and recommend options for sourcing new content

- Develop editorial workflow for publishing, approving, and removing content from sites

- Ensure content management systems are developed to meet publishing requirements
- Evaluate opportunities to reuse or streamline content across site
- Create content matrix containing asset-level detail, including metadata values that govern content behavior (placement within site structure, geographic distribution, translations)
- Engage in iterative content writing process, negotiating input and revisions from multiple subject matter experts
- Manage day-to-day operations of the content team, including setting priorities, assigning resources, and ensuring goals are achieved
- Uphold and evangelize content quality standards
- Work well as a team member of a large account, understanding how a team operates and what is expected in critiques and team meetings

- Perform creative thinking balancing technical feasibility and cool possibilities
- Create taxonomies and metadata frameworks for grouping and tagging content
- Ensure content conforms to Search Engine Optimization best practices
- Oversee content migrations and preparing documentation to do so
- Work with staff in various departments to ensure that content design is user-centric and consistent in style, format, and quality
- Perform business analysis and contribute to strategy development
- Efficiently interact with clients
- Identify/document WCMS content types
- Serve as consultant to project managers in sizing and scoping of content-related activities

The Web Content Strategist's Bible

# Appendix C – Abbreviations

AJAX – asynchronous JavaScript and XML

CMS – content management system

Gif – graphics interchange format

HTML – hypertext markup language

IA – information architect

JPEG – joint photographic experts group

ME – managing editor

PM – project manager

RSS – really simple syndication

SME – subject matter expert

URL – uniform resource locator

WCMS – Web content management system

XML – extensible markup language

The Web Content Strategist's Bible

# Appendix D – Access to Online Bonus Material

The book started life as an online e-book. Part of the e-book package was online access to a number of templates that can greatly cut the amount of time it takes to create some of these Content Strategy documents.

The most popular template is the Content Matrix Excel template, but there are others and the list will continue to grow so I will not list them here.

There is also a mobile-device-compatible electronic version (PDF) of the book at the same location.

To gain access to the online bonus materials send an email to:

**contentstrategistbible@gmail.com**

The Web Content Strategist's Bible

# Index

---

The Web Content Strategist's Bible

## M

## N

## O

## P

proposals, 25

**R**

Ranking Position, 150

Readability, 69

Readiness Analysis, 81

re-design websites, 27

**redirect**, 125

removing content from the website, 125

resume, 178

resume magic words, 178

*S*

samples of your work, 179

Scanability, 70

Search Engine Optimization, 144

search engines, 144

**Search logs**, 148

SEO, 144

SEO techniques, 152

Separating Content from Presentation, 165

Specifying Languages and Countries, 135

sponsor, 28

standards for grammatical usage, 99

static content, 27

Supporting Research, 186

*T*

Technical Architect, 29

**Technical Lead**, 29

technical writer, 13

The Web Content Strategist's Bible